Banjo Picking Tunes

BEAUTIFUL AMERICAN AIRS & BALLADS

by Lluís Gómez

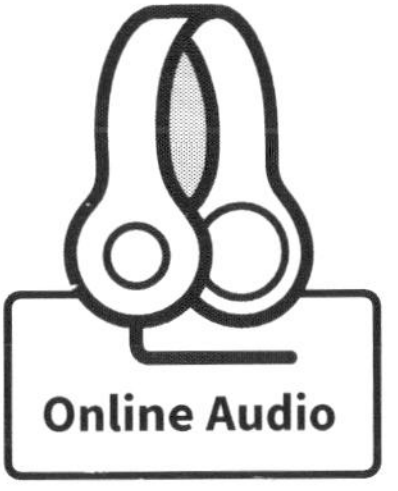

To access the online audio recording go to:
WWW.MELBAY.COM/30906MEB

The Prucha Spirit Jason Burleson Signature Model banjo cover image courtesy of Prucha Bluegrass Instruments.

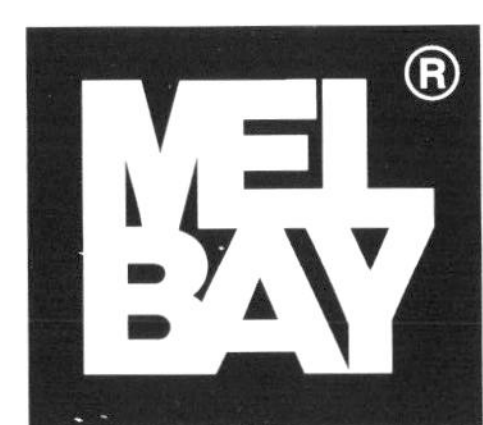

WWW.MELBAY.COM

Preface

This book presents a collection of 25 North American melodies arranged for 5-string banjo solo. Some of the pieces by have historical themes; for example, William Bay's "Trail of Tears" recalls the forced removal of Native Americans from their ancestral lands to designated reservations. This occurred between 1830 and 1850. As so many died along the route from exposure, disease and starvation, the journey became known as "The Trail of Tears".

"Black Sunday" refers to a severe dust storm that occurred on April 14,1935 in the Oklahoma Panhandle. It was one of the worst storms of its kind in American history and left a trail of agricultural and economic destruction. This musical setting reflects the deprivation and tragedy common during the Great Depression.

Any collection of American ballads would be incomplete without settings of the beautiful melodies penned by Stephen Foster. Several of his tunes are included here, with "Beautiful Dreamer", "Darling Nellie Gray", "I Dream of Jeanie with the Light Brown Hair", and "Hard Times, Come Again No More" among them.

Tablature

The music in this book is intended for intermediate to advanced players who read 5-string banjo tablature. If you are not familiar with this system of notation, there are countless tutorials on the Internet that explain it. All the tunes in this collection are arranged in standard gDGBD banjo tuning. The companion online recording can be used to further clarify the objective of the tablature.

Some of these tunes are arranged in uncommon banjo keys; for example, "Beautiful Dreamer" is in the key of E♭, "Hard Times, Come Again No More" is in the key of A and "I Dream of Jeanie with the Light Brown Hair" is in the key of B♭—all without retuning the banjo or using a capo. These keys may prove challenging, but you will learn a lot about the banjo fretboard. Another thing you will notice is that several chord shapes require extreme extensions of your left-hand fingers; these chords sound beautiful and are worth the effort but be prepared for some big stretches.

Fingerings

I didn't mark any of the left-hand fingerings that are commonly indicated in classical music notation; in general, these are natural hand and finger positions, and you will not have a hard time figuring them out. A lot of these positions consist of familiar chord forms but use a pencil to add whatever helps you play more fluently.

For the right hand, my approach is something else entirely; in fact, in the banjo world, right-hand fingerings are the subject of non-stop discussion. Over the years I have had many conversations with colleagues about the best way to play fiddle tunes—and it's a great topic!

For the tunes in this collection, I conceived and play my fingerings like a classical guitarist, so I may decide to play a succession of notes on the first string, alternating the index and middle fingers;

I know that the usual banjo rules don't apply here but it's my option, if only because I formally studied the classical guitar.

Using the Recordings

There are tempo suggestions on the page and recording for each piece, yet some may sound better to your ears either faster or slower. Like all new music, I suggest learning these pieces at a slow tempo before increasing the speed.

Record Yourself

I encourage you to record yourself in both audio and video media as a practice tool. We often overlook many details in the heat of the moment when playing. Retrospective viewing or listening provides evidence of how you are progressing with any piece. It may even alert you to some extraneous sounds.

The banjo provides lots of opportunities to make incidental noises, like your thumb pick hitting the head, or metal picks striking the metal strings. In sparse arrangements like some of the selections found in this book, those noises may show up in a more pronounced fashion when compared to a noisy bluegrass jam. *Awareness* is the first step to eliminating these problems. Isolating the right hand in practice at very slow tempos will help clear up such issues.

Interpretation

As you learn these pieces, the practice of interpretation becomes more important—i.e., making musical decisions beyond what the tablature indicates. In the Information Age, we can stream different performances of the same piece of music. Notice that while each musician is playing the same notes, the performances are distinctive; these differences are due to the artists' individual interpretations of the piece.

In classical music, there are often indications on the sheet music telling musicians how to play the piece in terms of tempo, dynamics, articulation, fingering, and even what emotions to exude. These cues help us to play the music as the composer intended, not to mention giving heart and soul to the music. Aside from tempo indications, those cues are not provided here. Your task is to listen to the pieces on YouTube or other recordings as played by various artists and make your own artistic decisions about interpretation.

Acknowledgments

Thanks to Maribel Rivero for her help and ideas with this book and especially for her love and support over the years. Thanks also to my many banjo colleagues and students around the world, and an extra special thank you to the staff at Mel Bay Publications: William, Sharon, Joanne, Julie, and Stephen.

Recorded by Lluís Gómez at Dotze Contes Studio.
Mastering by Jordi "Kako" Vericat at JK Music.
Lluís Gómez plays and endorses Prucha Banjos.

Contents

Title	Page	Audio
Aura Lee	5	1
Beautiful Dreamer	6	2
Black Is the Color of My True Love's Hair	8	3
Black Sunday	10	4
Darling Nellie Gray	11	5
Hard Times, Come Again No More	12	6
I Dream of Jeanie with the Light Brown Hair	13	7
In the Pines	14	8
Johnny Has Gone for a Soldier	15	9
Just A-Wearyn' for You	16	10
Just Before the Battle, Mother	18	11
Land of Rest	20	12
Lorena	22	13
Mighty Lak' a Rose	23	14
Paper of Pins	24	15
Prairie Sunset	26	16
Pretty Peggy - O	28	17
Shady Grove	29	18
Shenandoah	30	19
The Lonesome Dove	31	20
The Long Road	32	21
The Old Country	34	22
The Old Homestead	36	23
To a Wild Rose	37	24
Trail of Tears	38	25
About the Author	40	

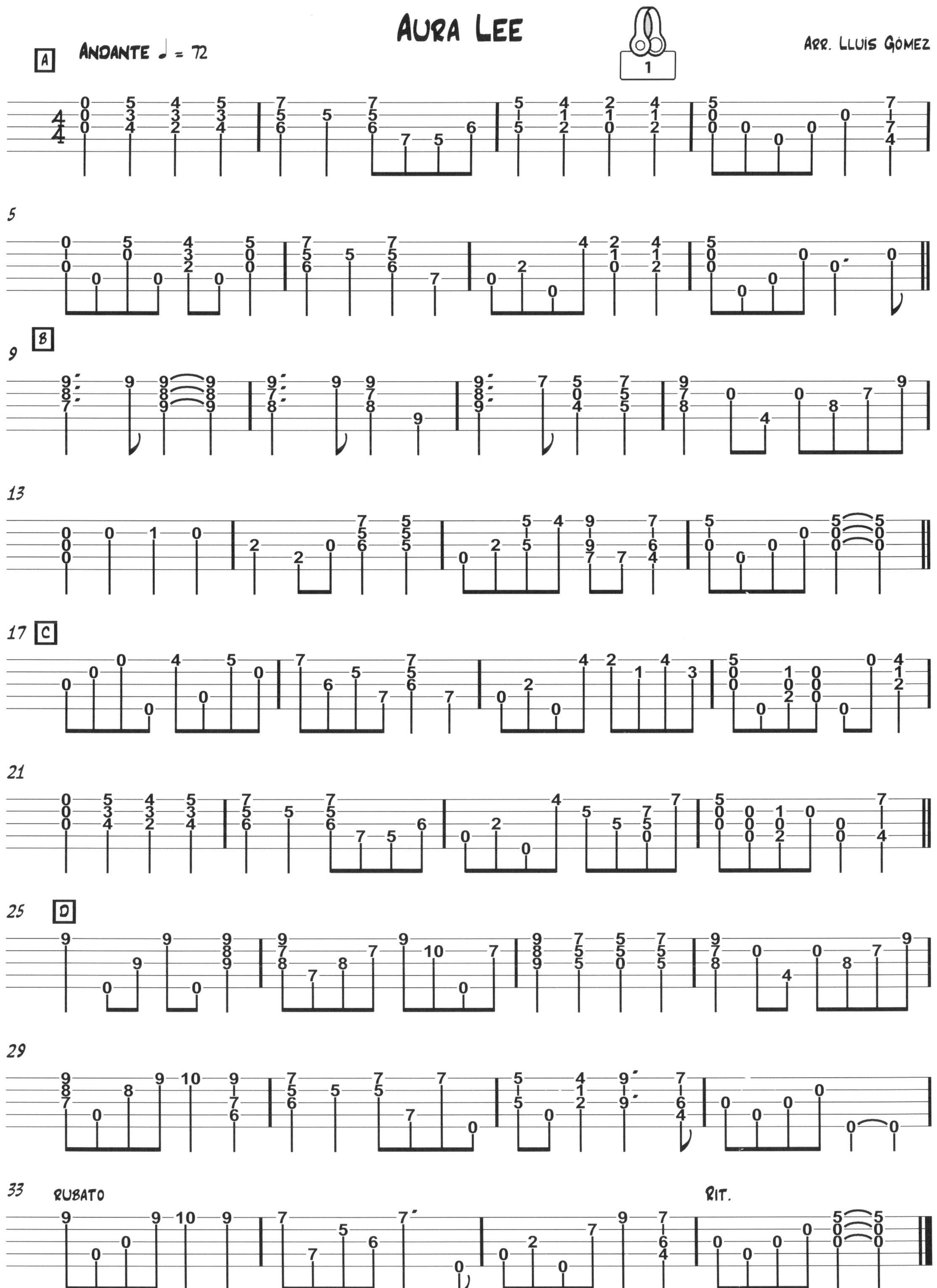

Aura Lee
Andante ♩ = 72
Arr. Lluis Gómez
A
B
C
D
Rubato
Rit.

BEAUTIFUL DREAMER

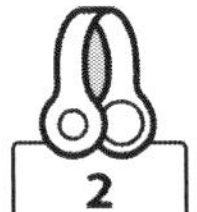

STEPHEN FOSTER
ARR. LLUIS GÓMEZ

ANDANTE ♩ = 120

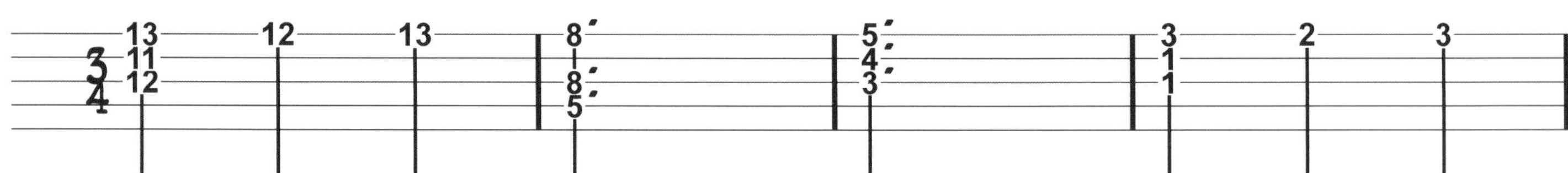

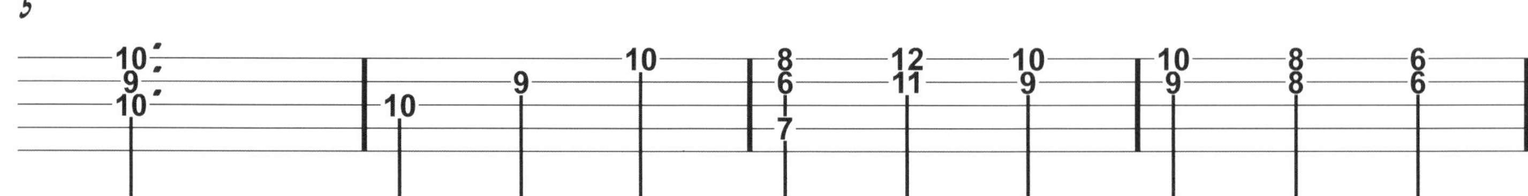

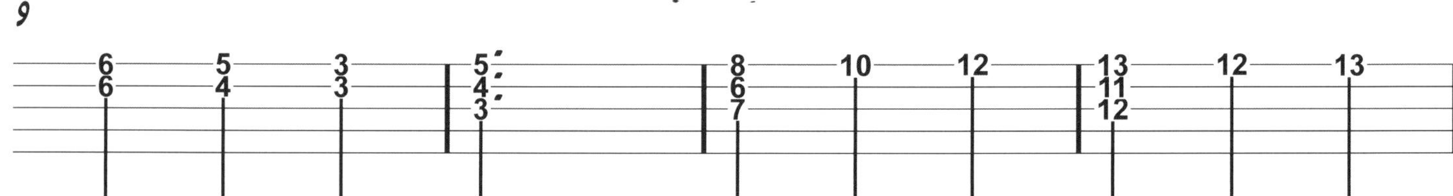

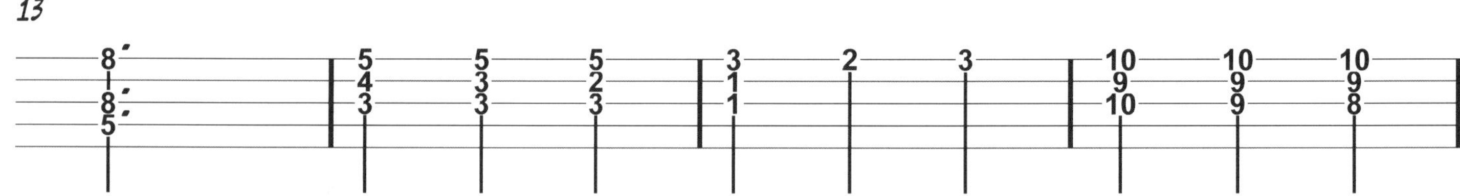

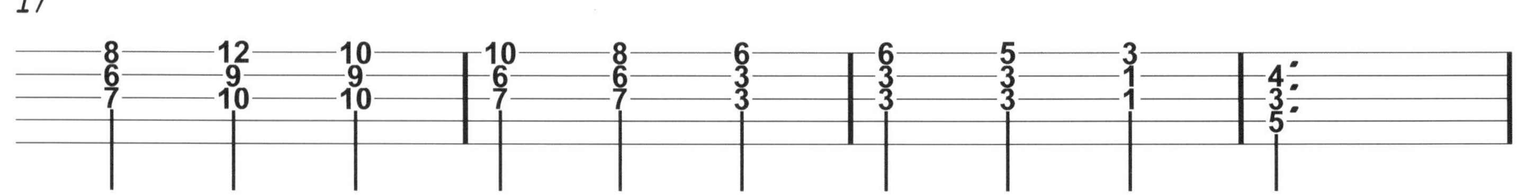

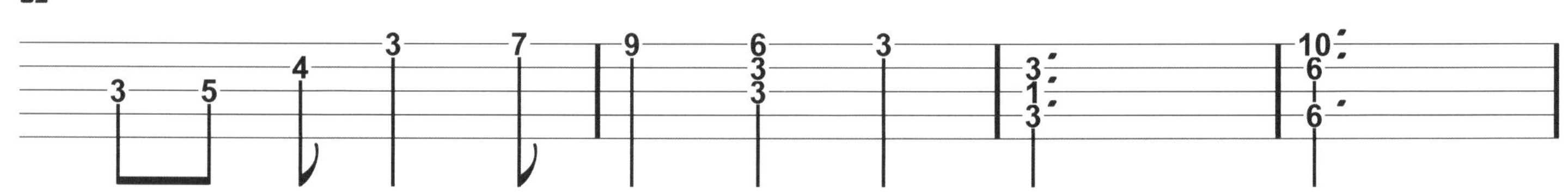

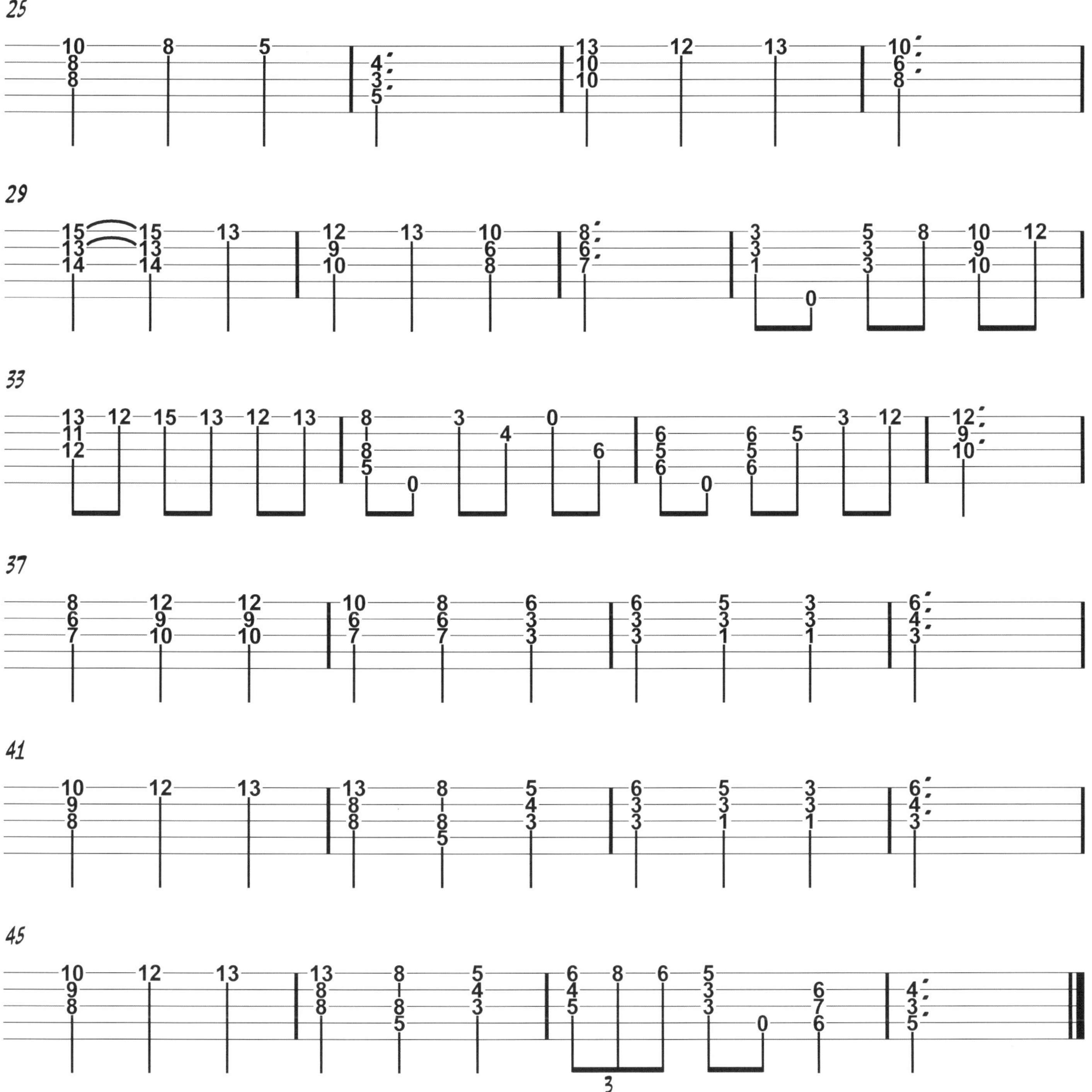

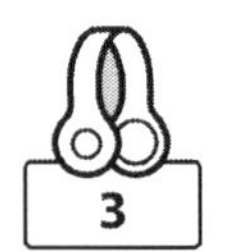

Black Is the Color of My True Love's Hair

Arr. Lluis Gómez

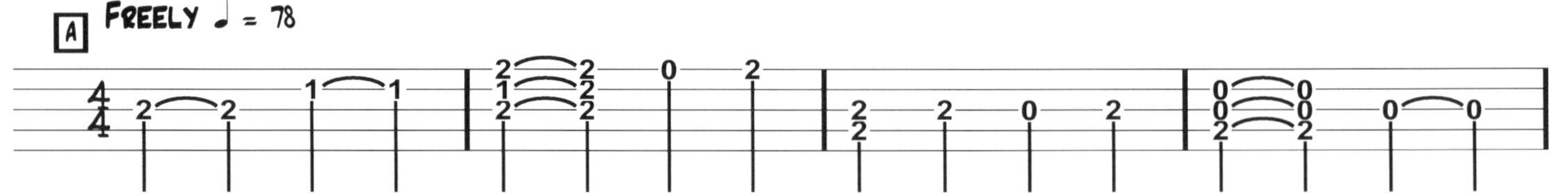

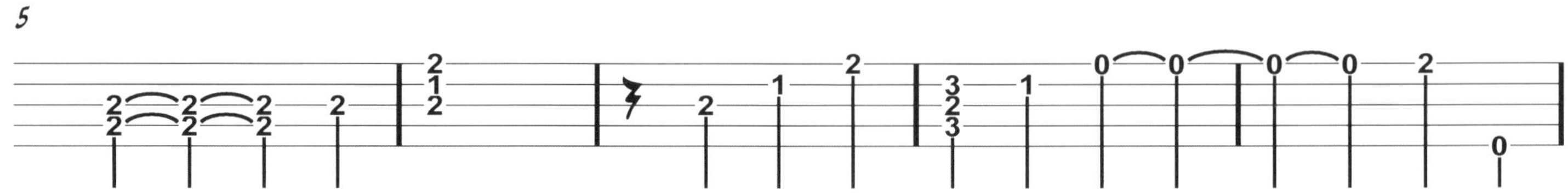

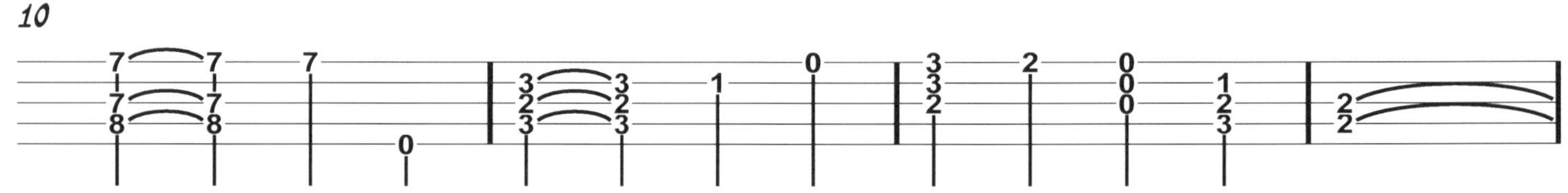

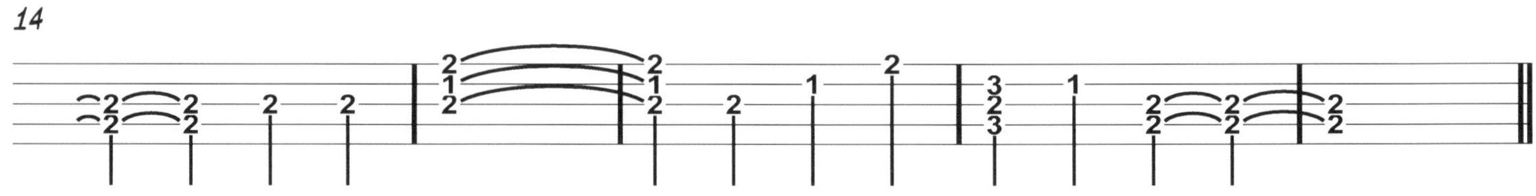

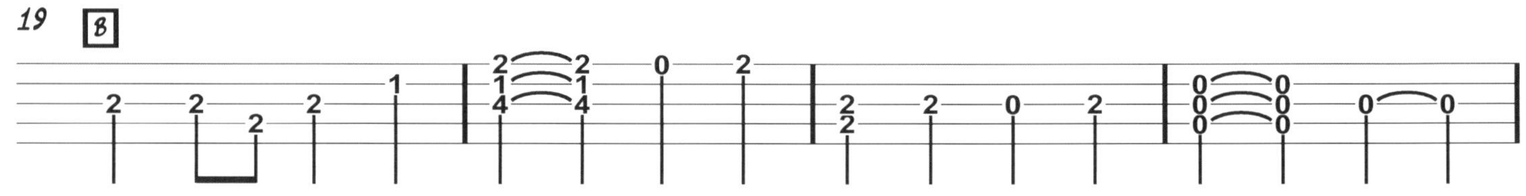

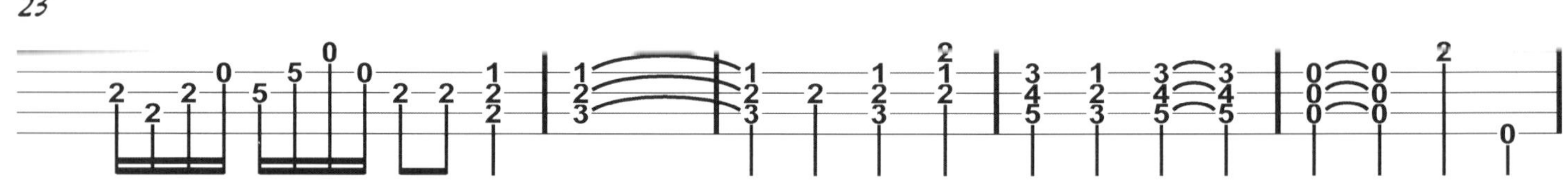

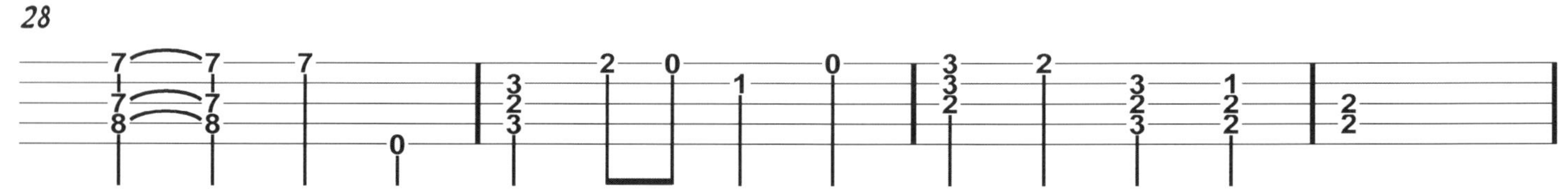

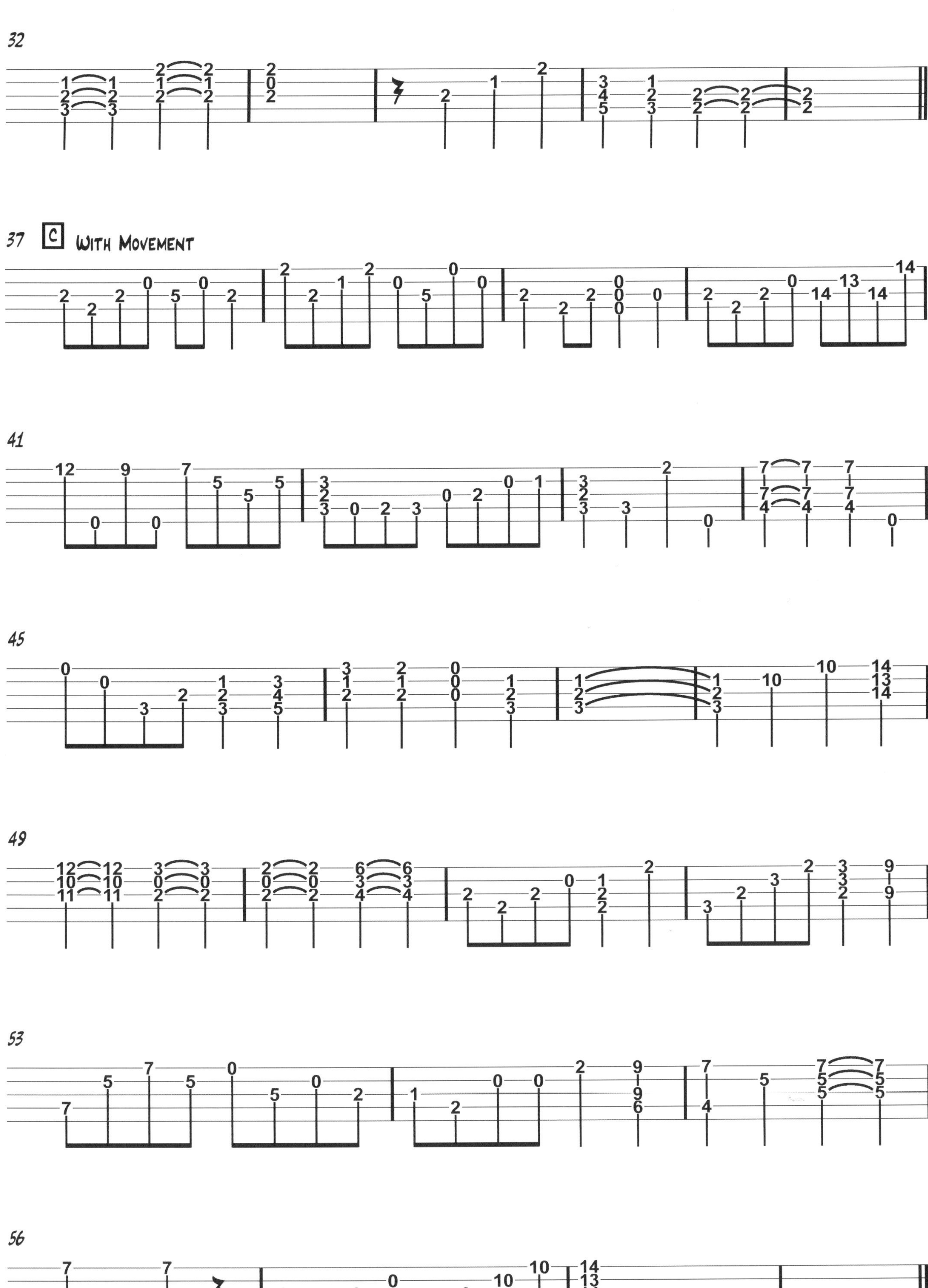
C
With Movement

Black Sunday
Oklahoma, April 14, 1935

Andante ♩ = 74

William Bay
Arr. Lluis Gomez

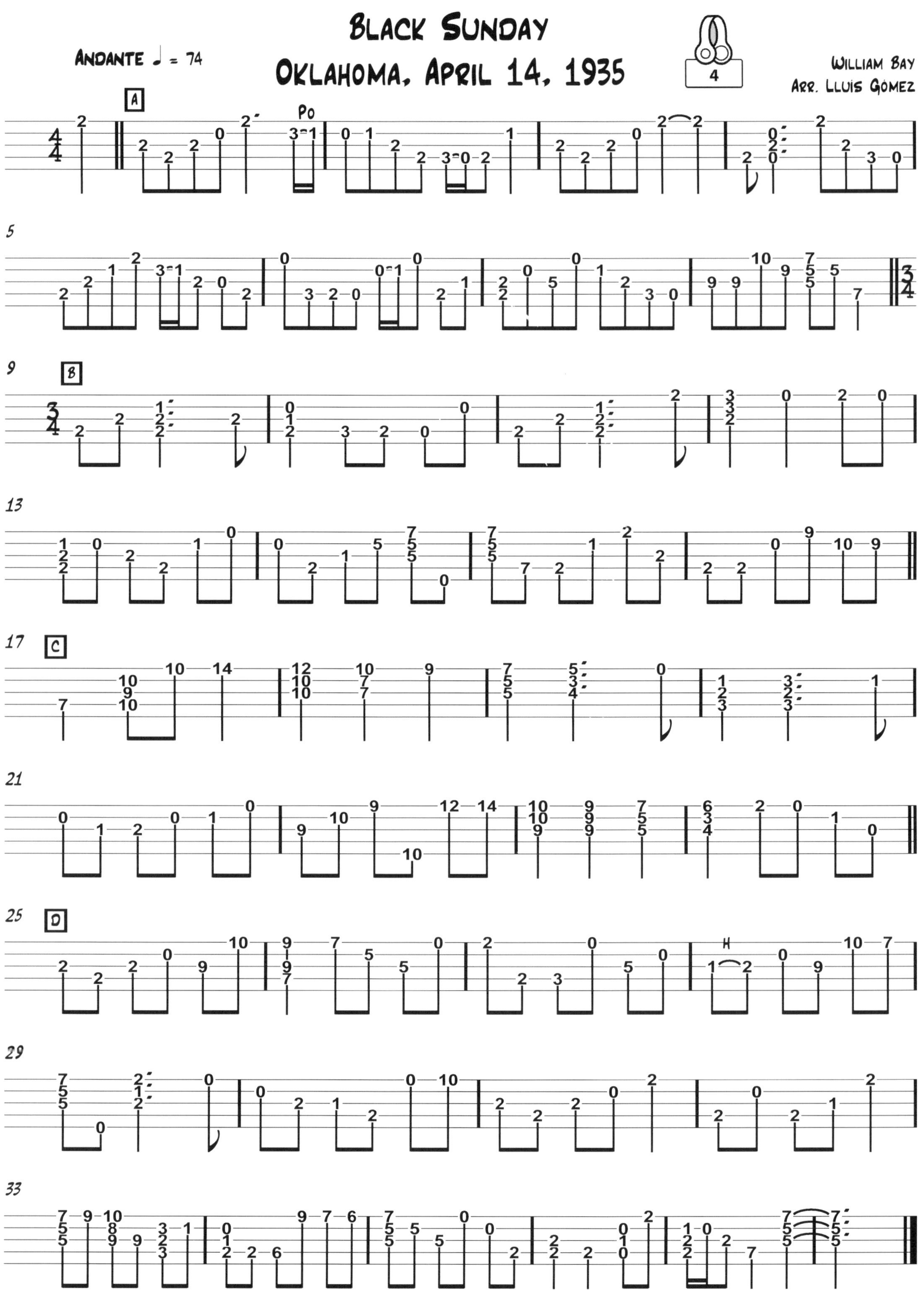

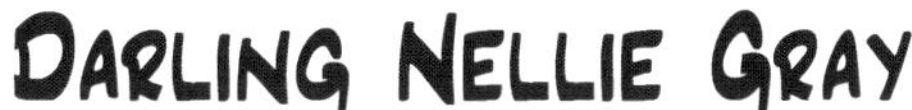

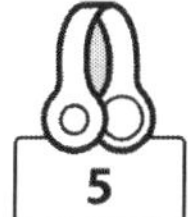

Stephen Foster
Arr. Lluis Gomez

Freely ♩ = 74

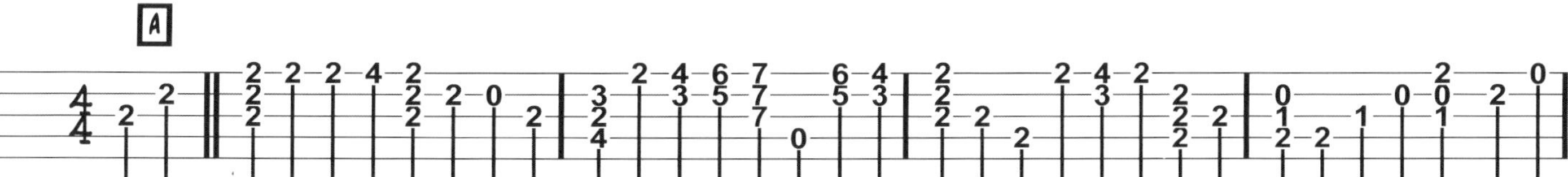

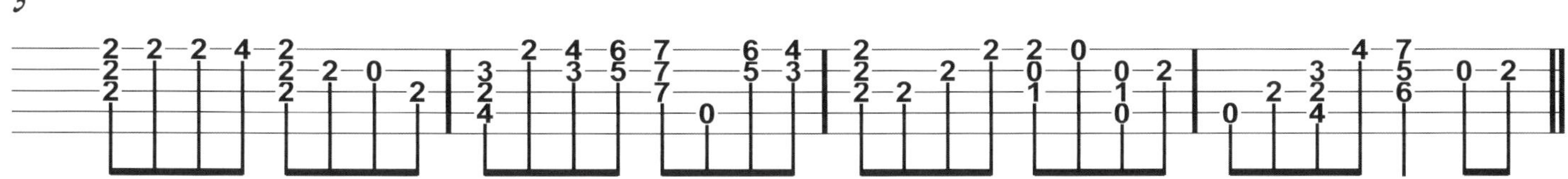

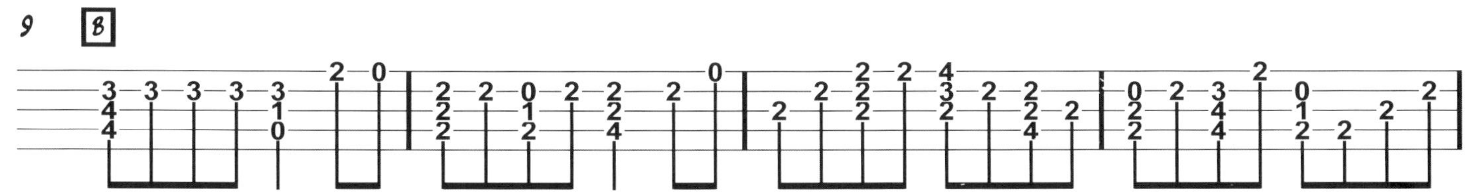

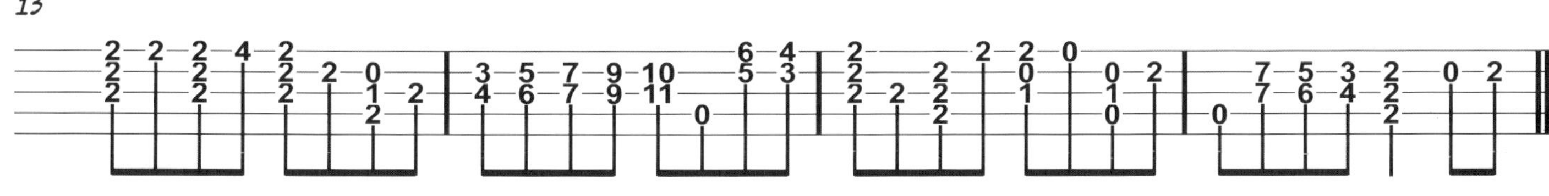

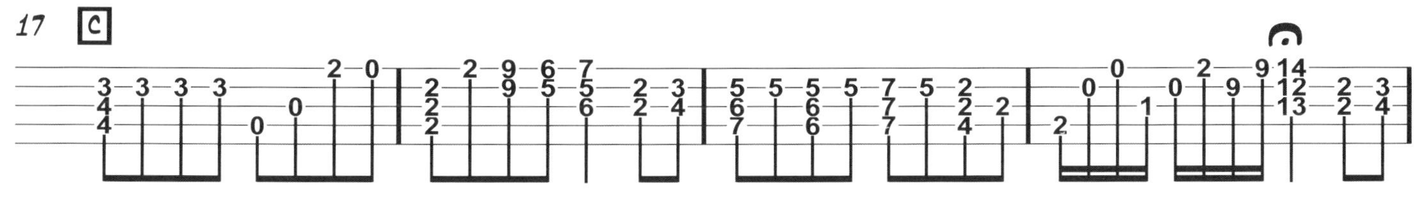

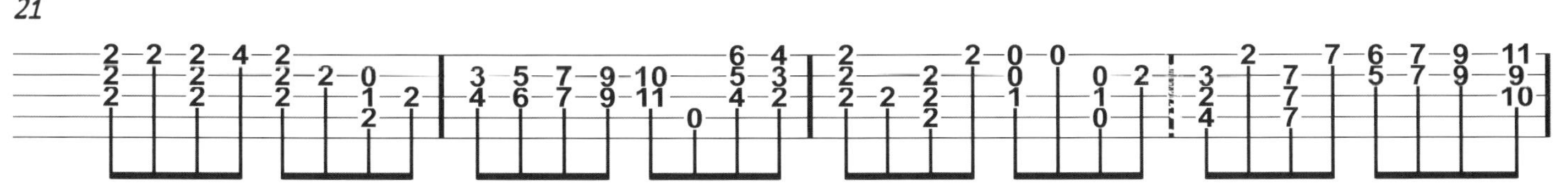

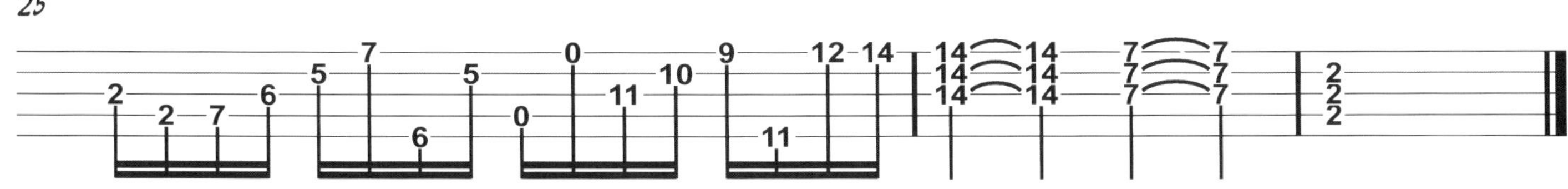

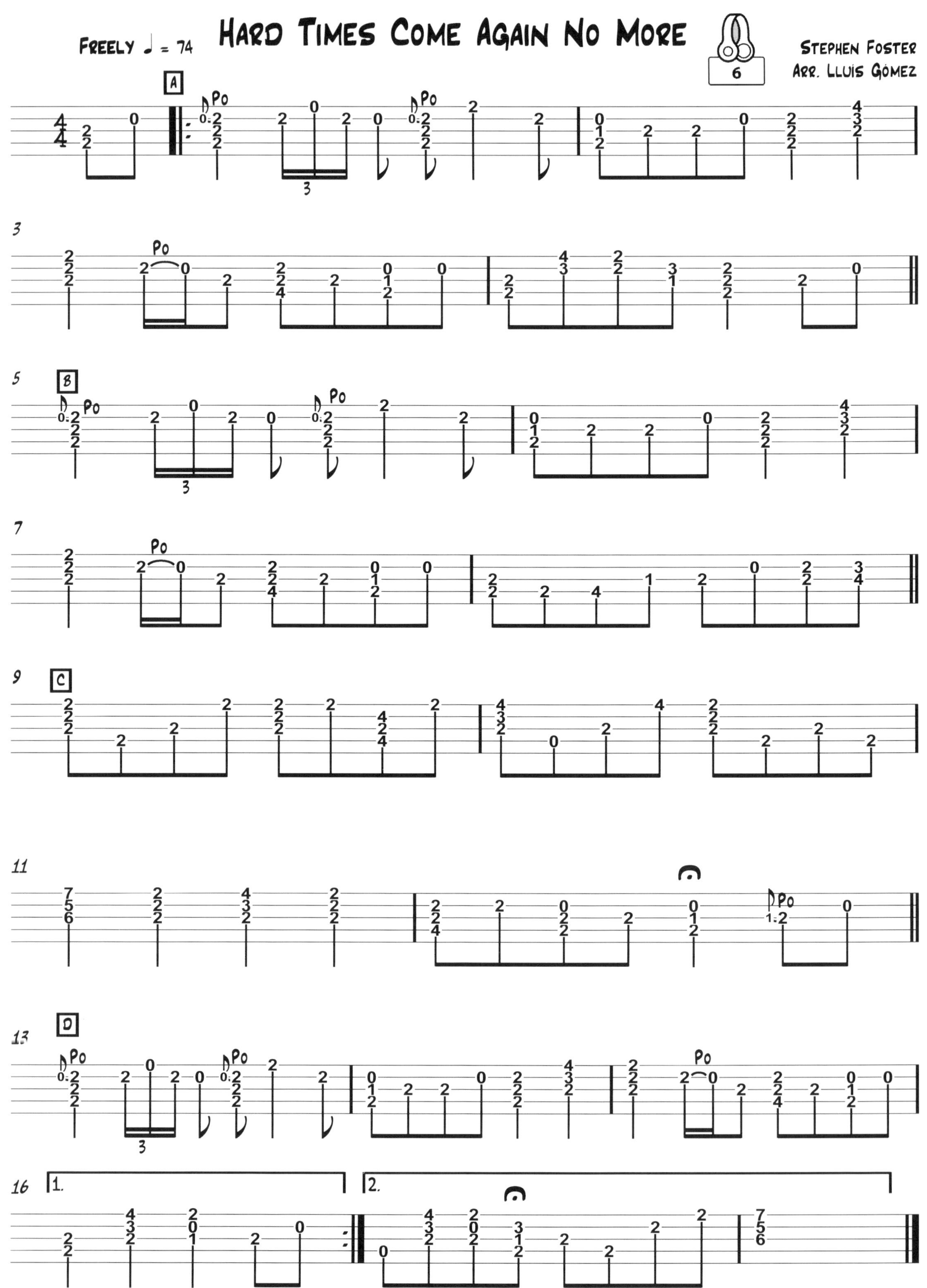
Freely ♩ = 74
Hard Times Come Again No More
6
Stephen Foster
Arr. Lluis Gómez
A
B
C
D
1.
2.

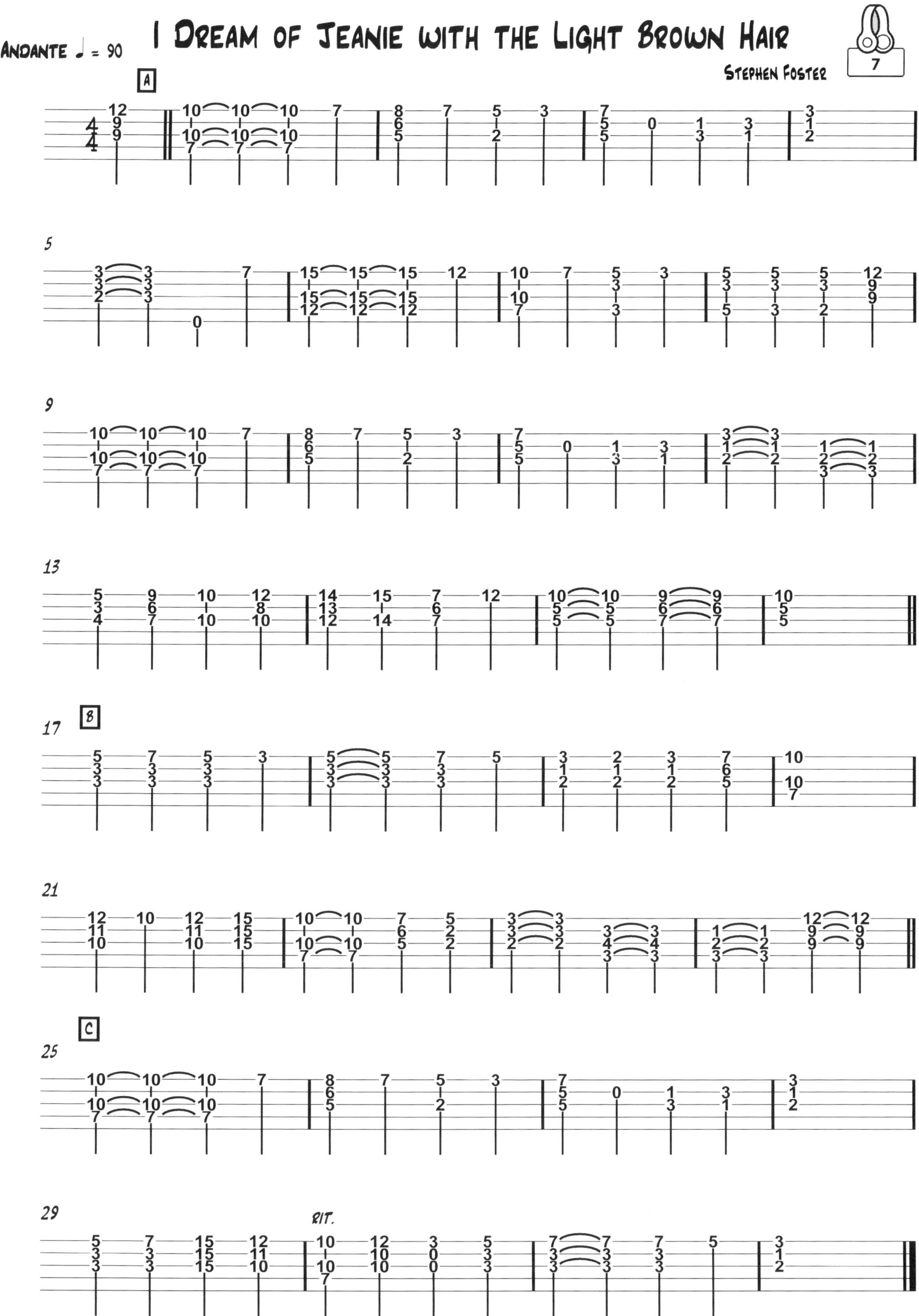
I Dream of Jeanie with the Light Brown Hair
Andante ♩ = 90
Stephen Foster
7
A
B
C
rit.

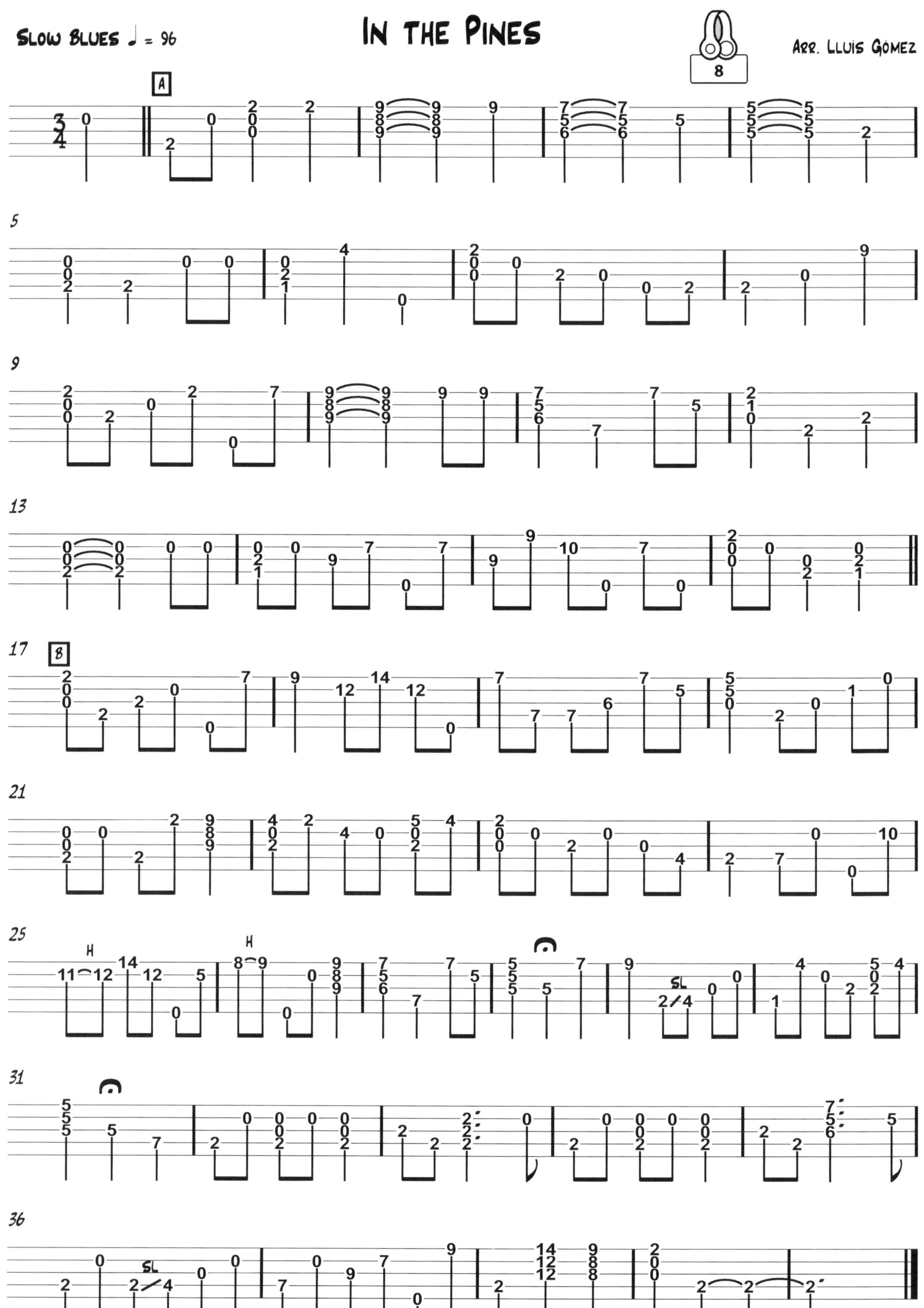
Slow Blues ♩ = 96
In the Pines
Arr. Lluis Gomez
8
A
B

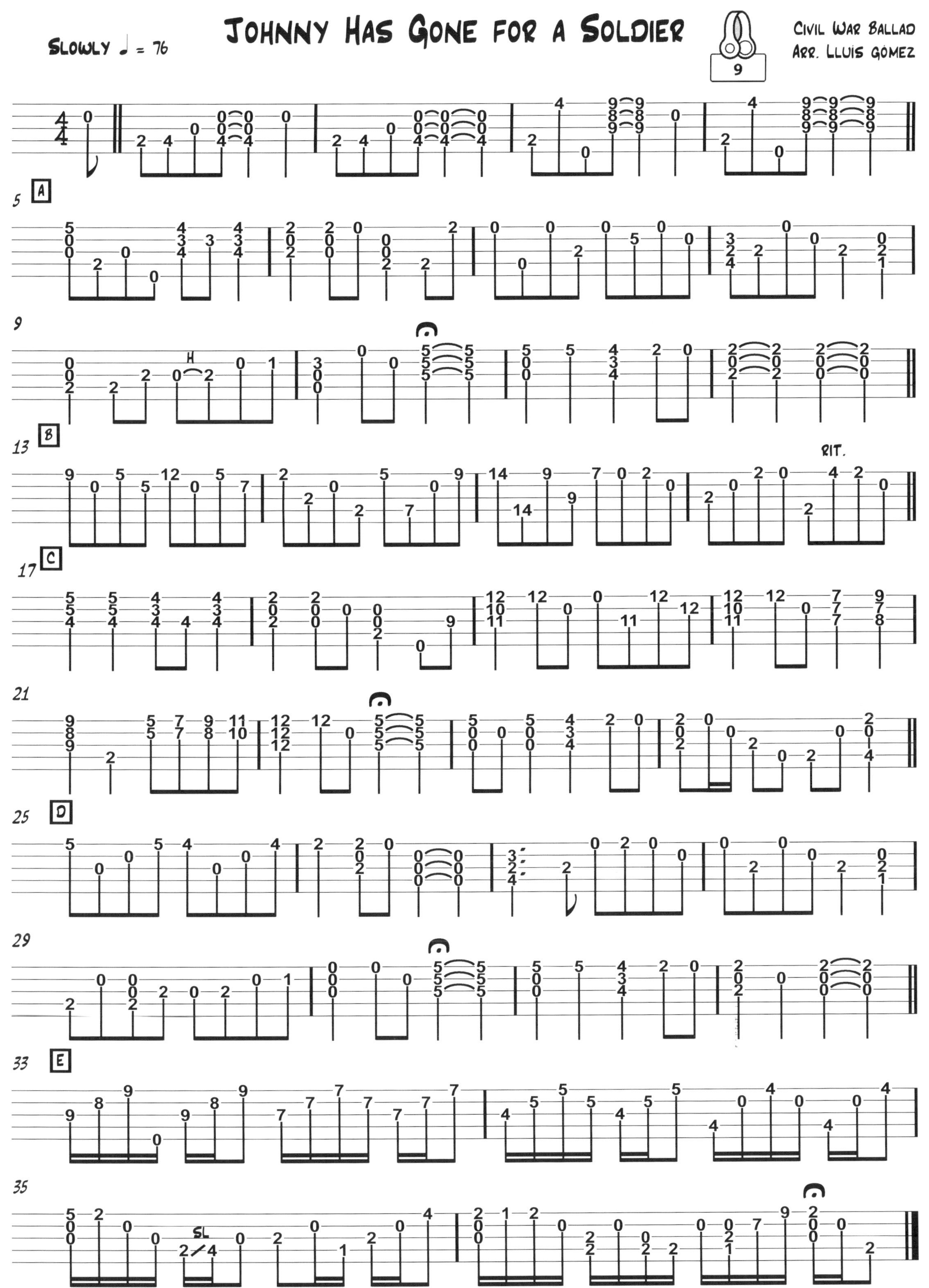
Johnny Has Gone for a Soldier
Slowly ♩ = 76
Civil War Ballad
Arr. Lluis Gomez
A
B
C
D
E
Rit.

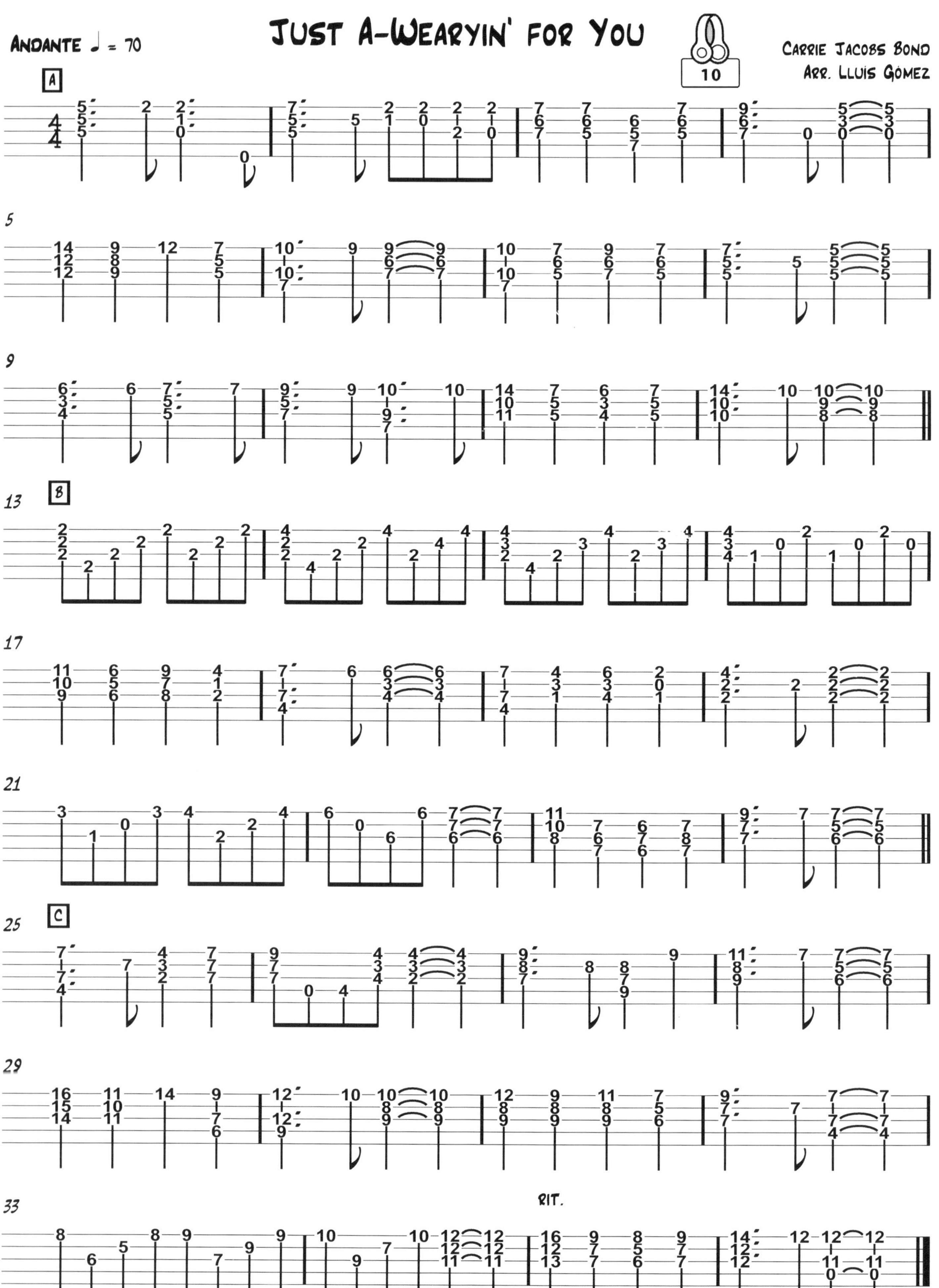
Andante ♩ = 70
Just A-Wearyin' for You
10
Carrie Jacobs Bond
Arr. Lluis Gomez
A
B
C
rit.

This page has been left blank to avoid an awkward page turn.

Just Before the Battle, Mother

Civil War Song
by George F. Root
Arr. Lluis Gómez

Tenderly ♩ = 78

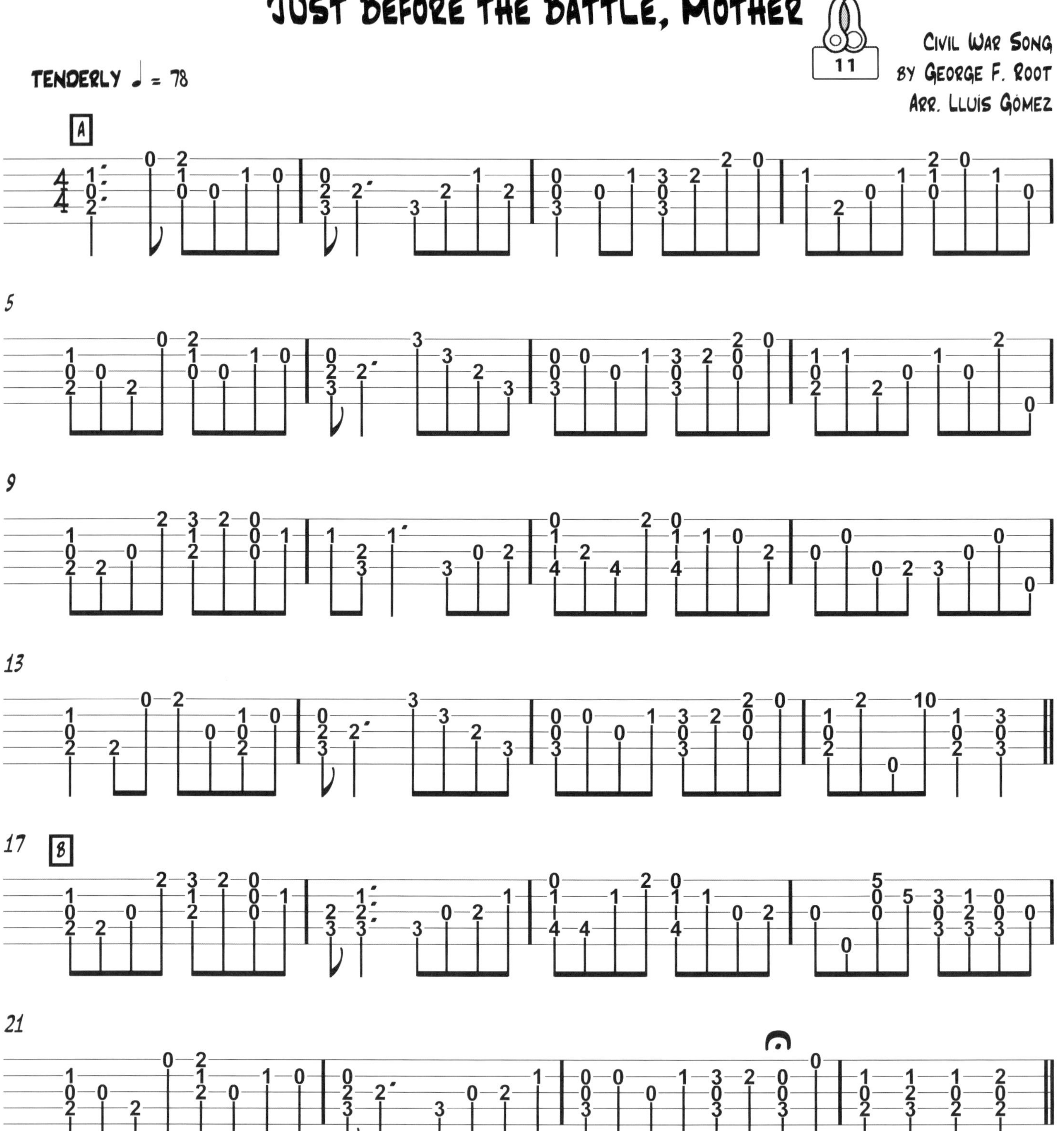

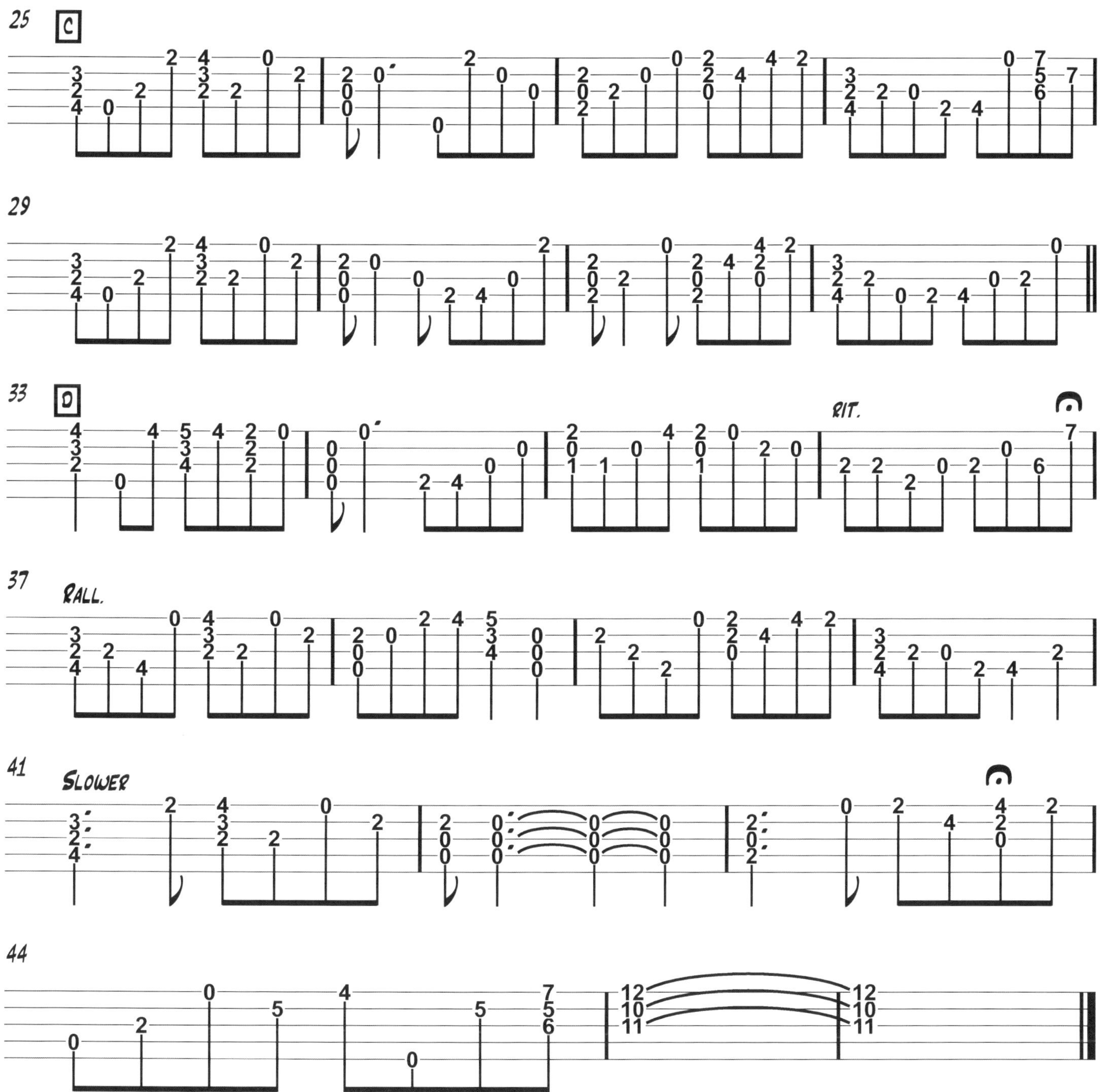
25
C
29
33
D
RIT.
37
RALL.
41
SLOWER
44

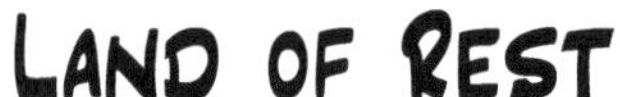

Early American Sacred Melody
Arr. Lluis Gomez

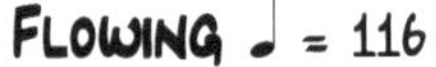

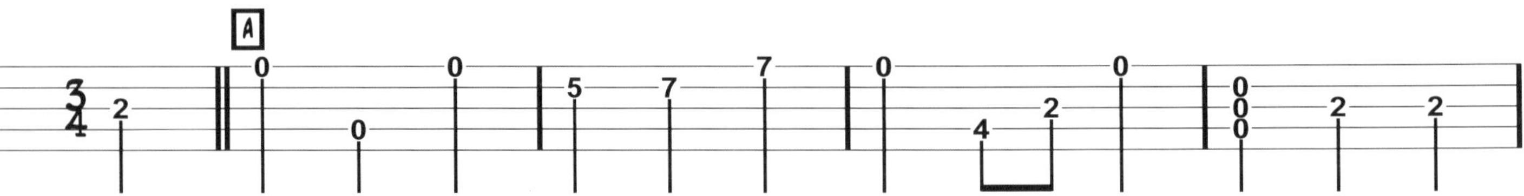

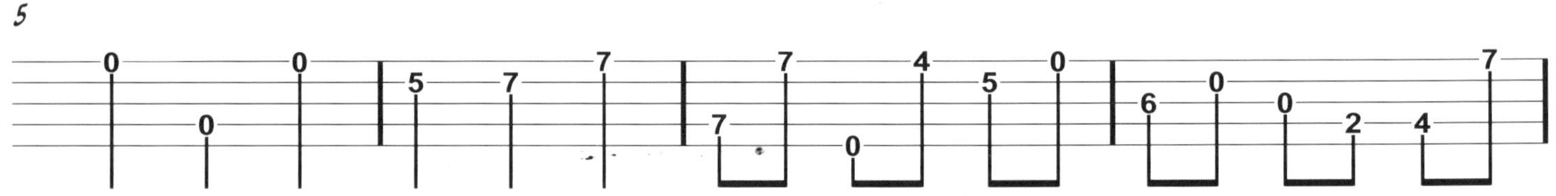

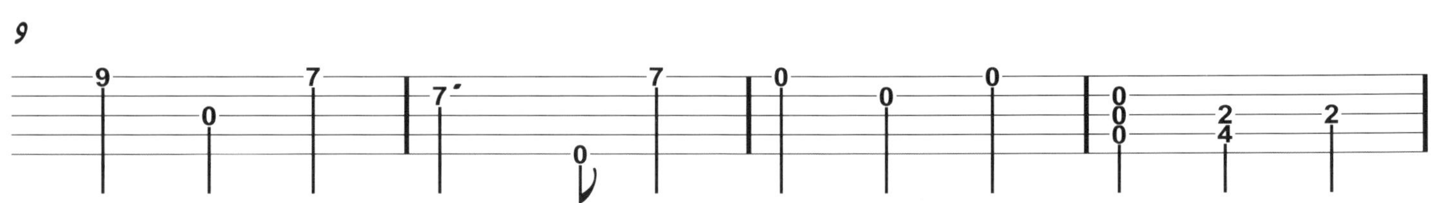

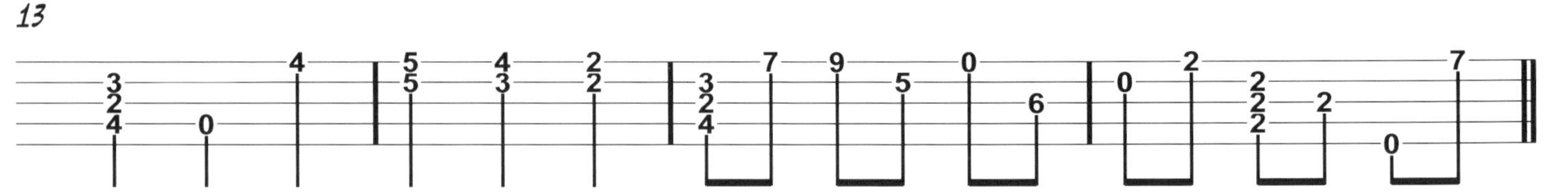

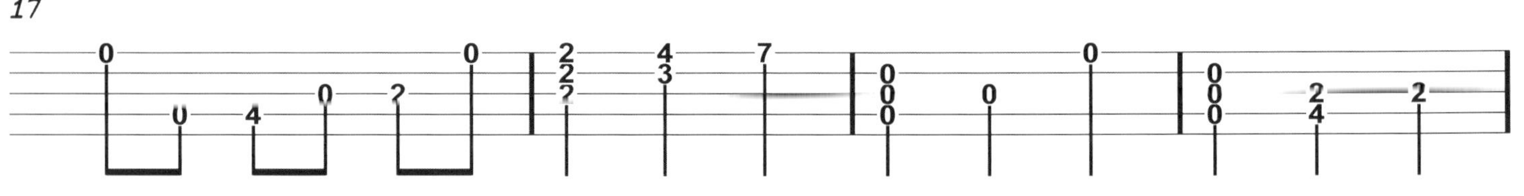

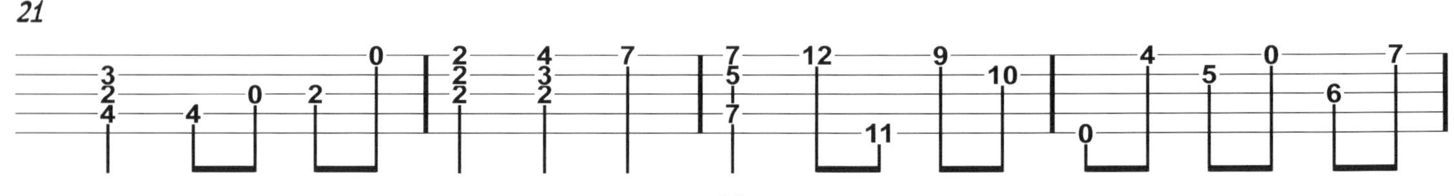

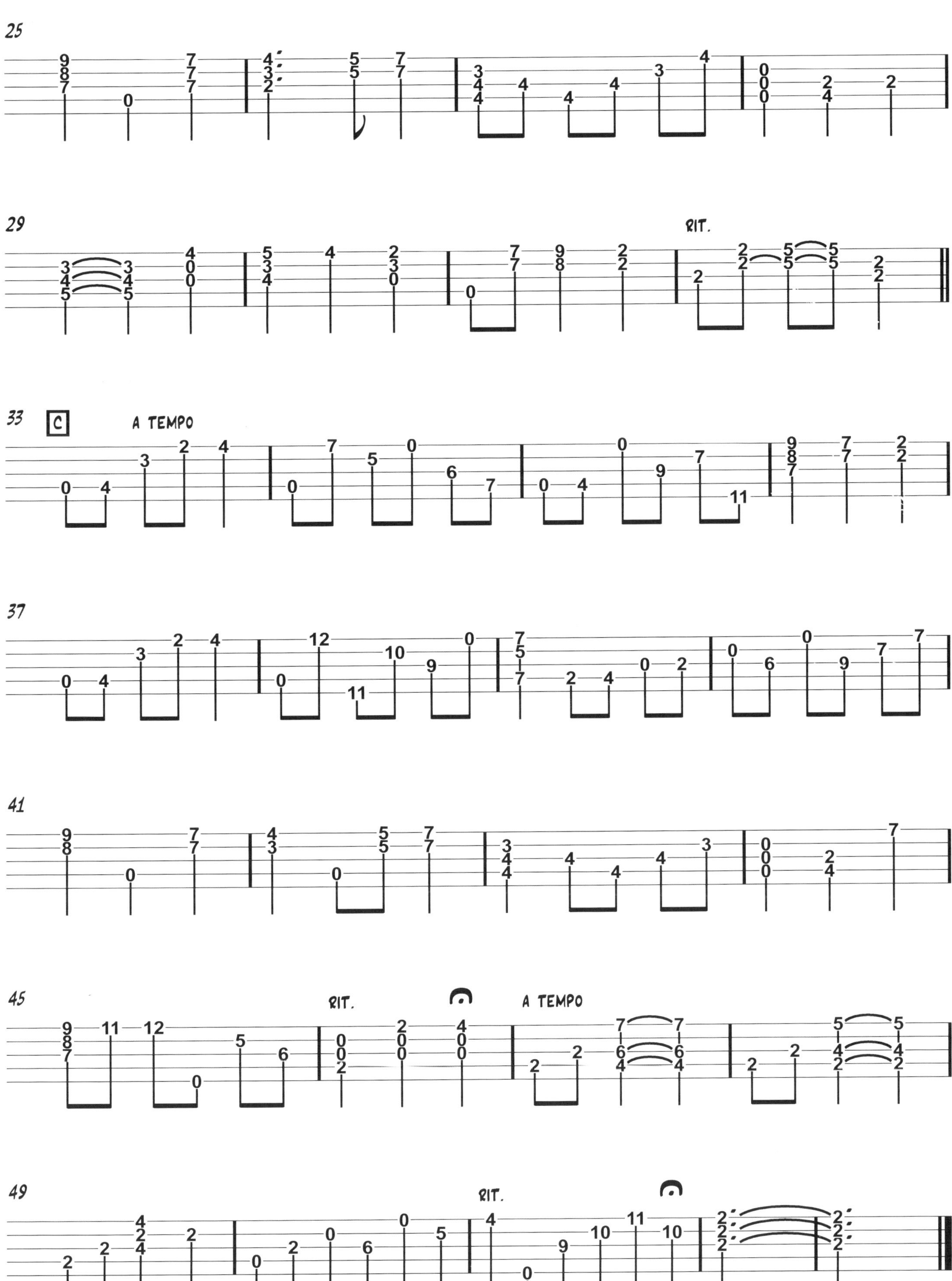
25
29
RIT.
33
C
A TEMPO
37
41
45
RIT.
A TEMPO
49
RIT.

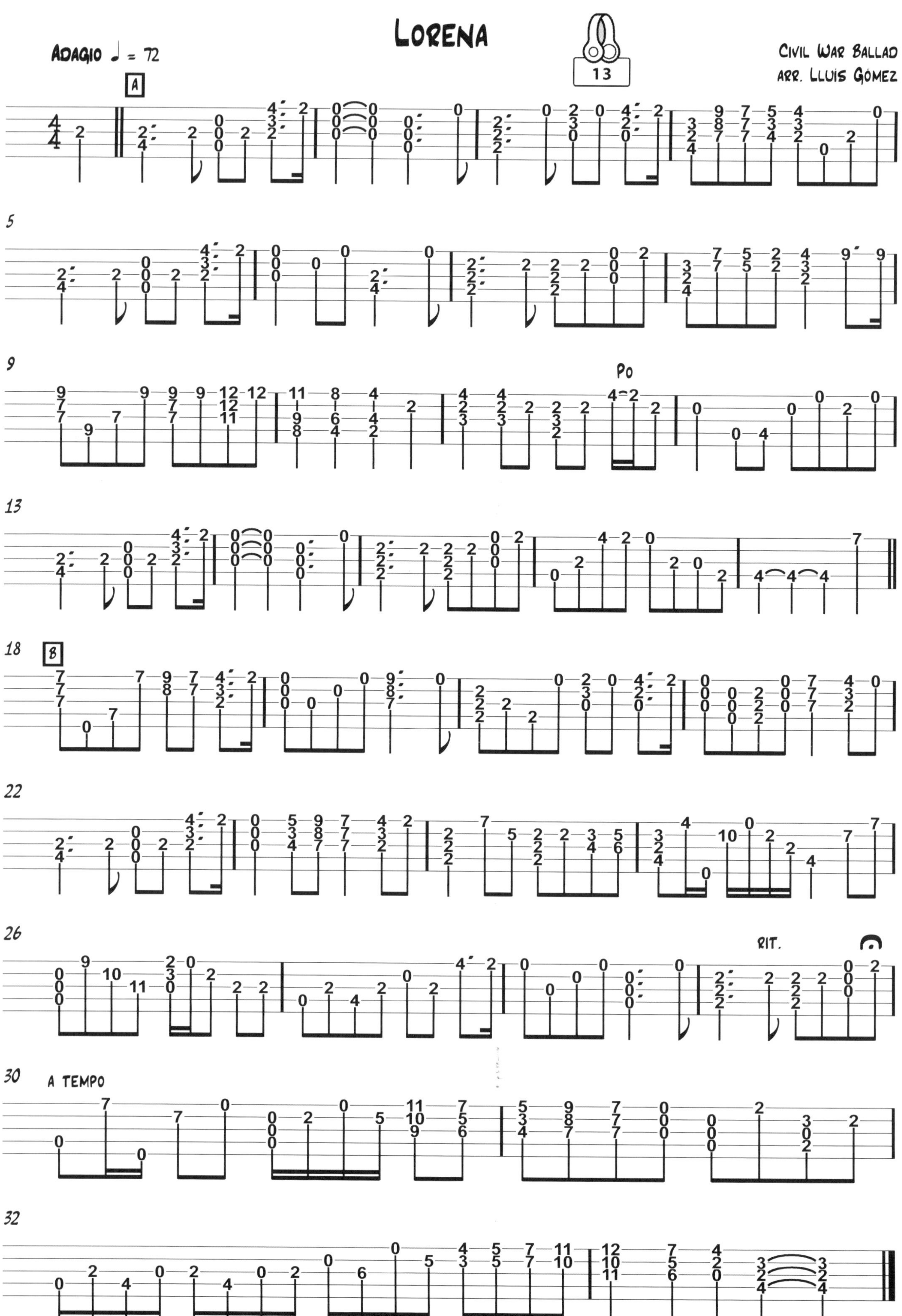
Lorena
Adagio ♩ = 72
Civil War Ballad
Arr. Lluis Gómez
13
A
B
Po
Rit.
A tempo

Mighty Lak' A Rose

Nevin
Arr. Lluís Gómez

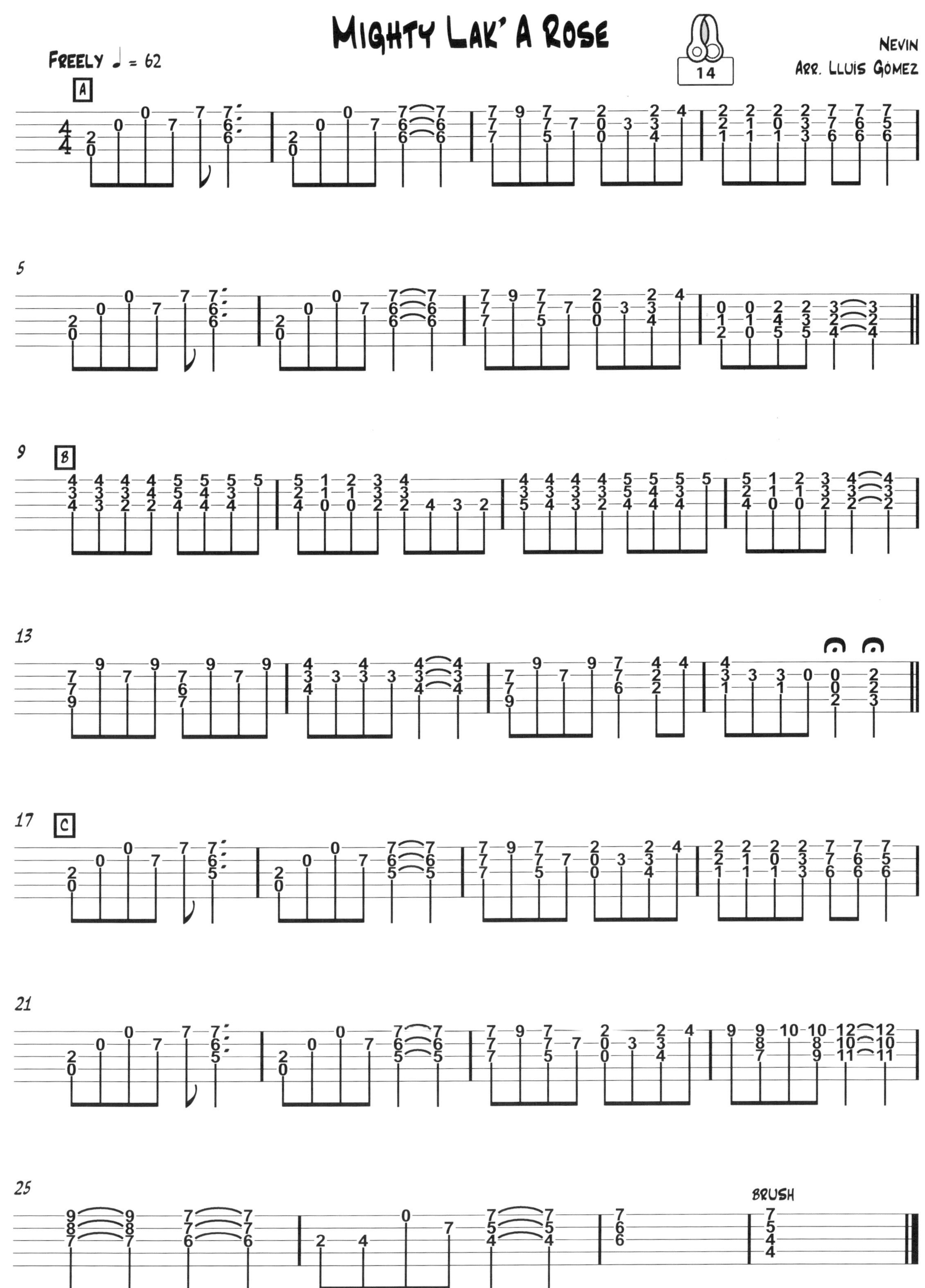

Paper of Pins

Moderately ♩ = 88

15

Arr. Lluis Gómez

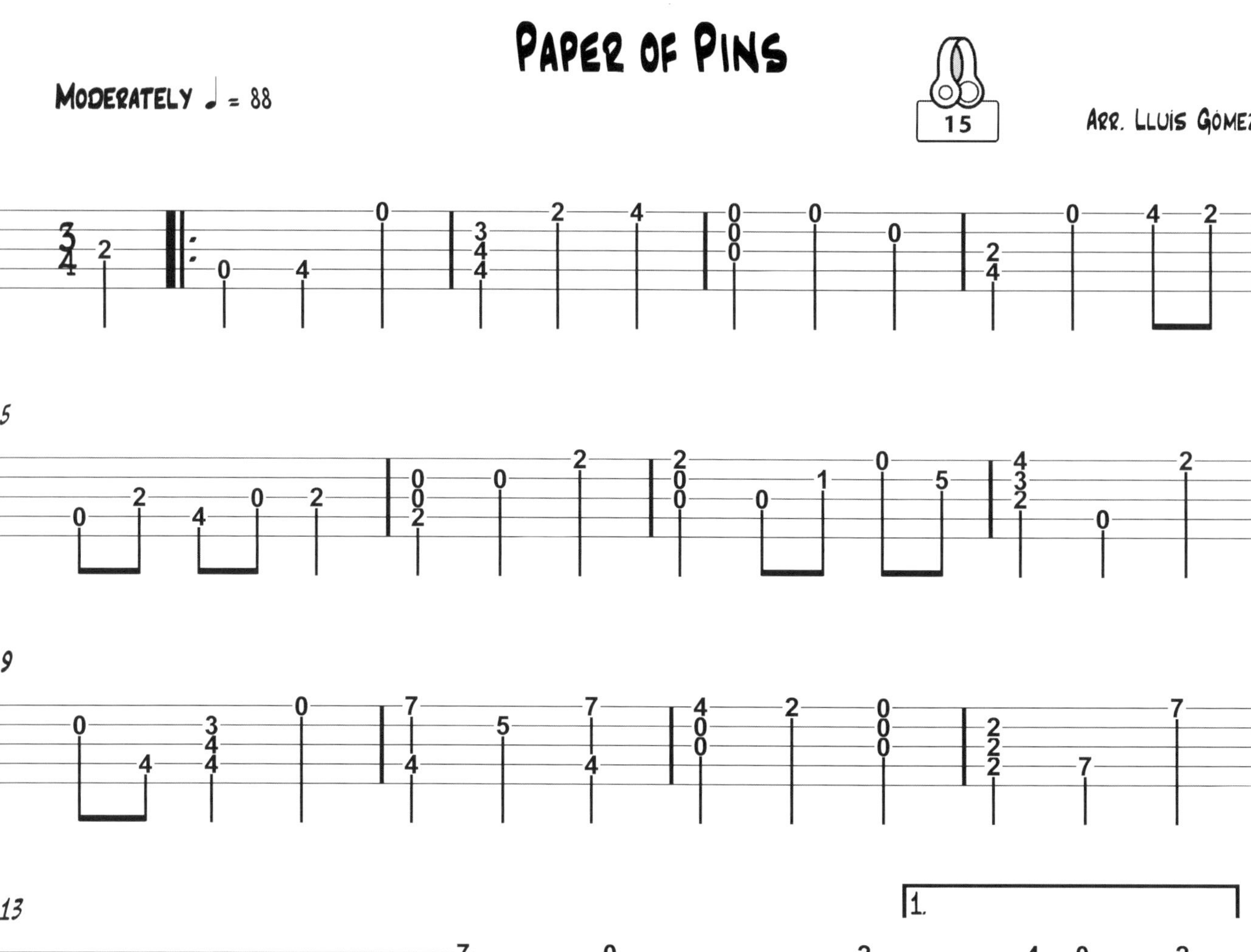

This page has been left blank to avoid an awkward page turn.

Prairie Sunset

Moderately ♩ = 90

16

William Bay
Arr. Lluis Gomez

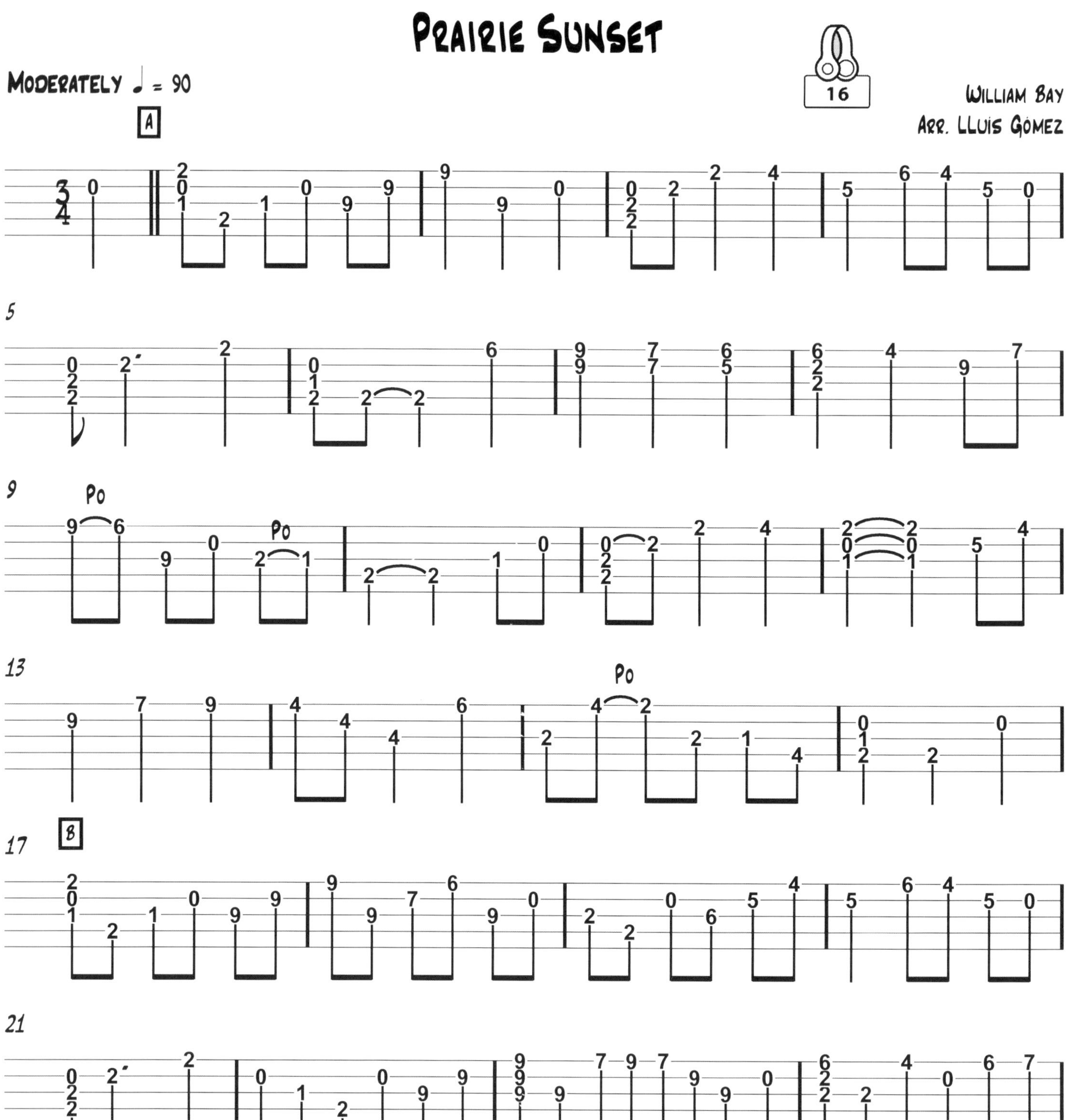

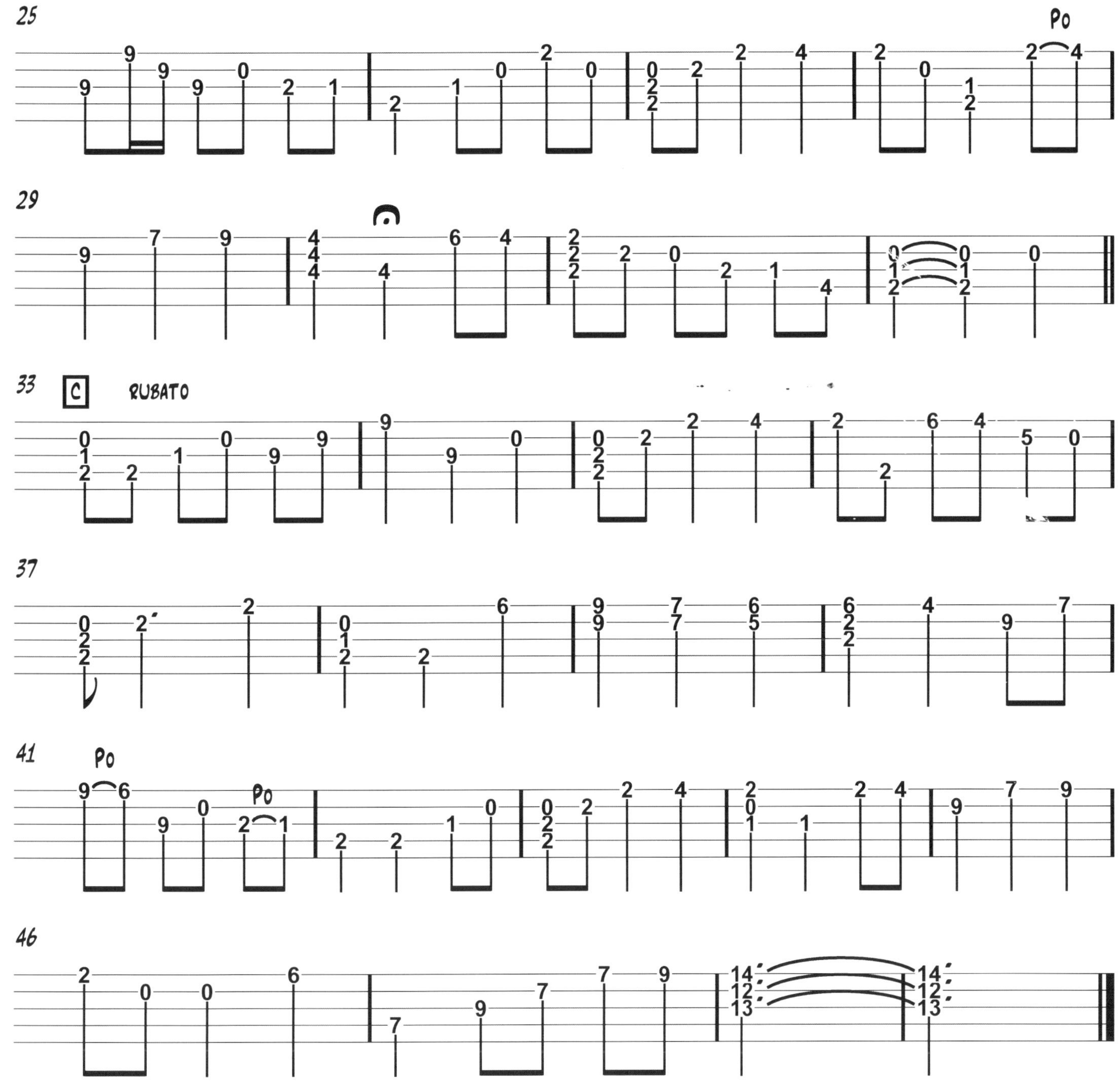
25
Po
29
33
C
RUBATO
37
41
Po
Po
46

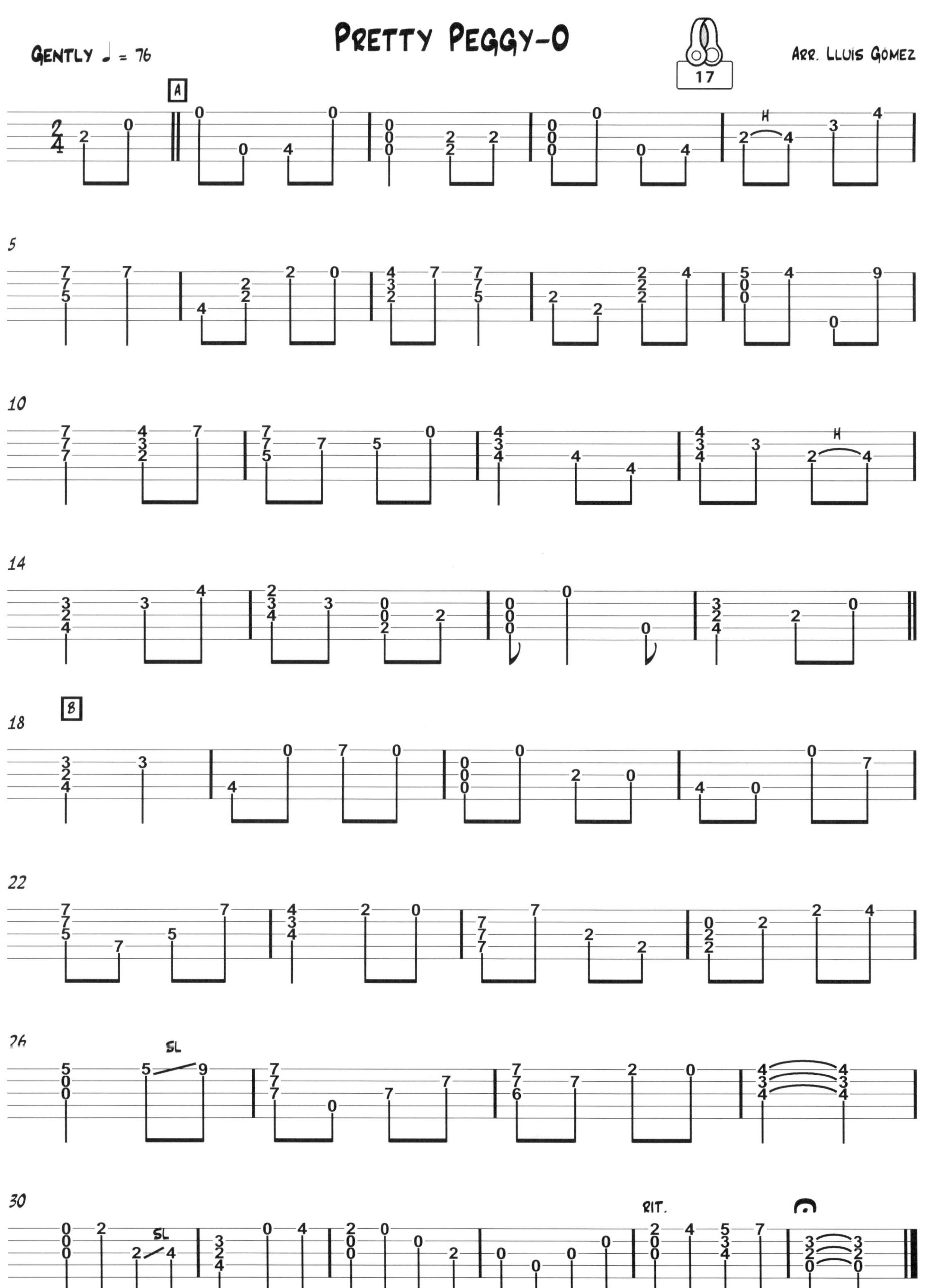
Pretty Peggy-O
Gently ♩ = 76
Arr. Lluis Gómez
17
A
H
B
SL
RIT.

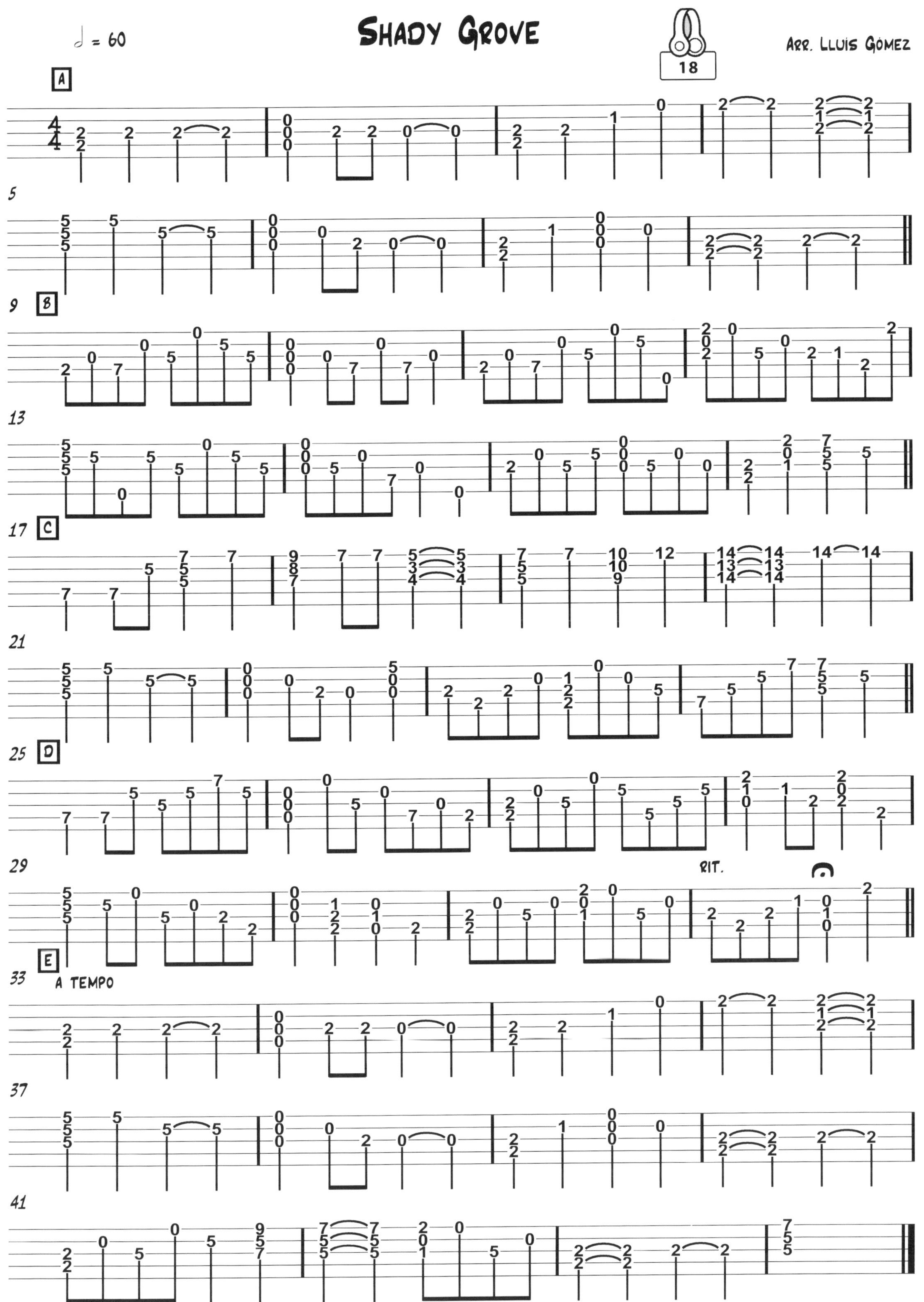

Shady Grove
= 60
18
Arr. Lluis Gómez
A
B
C
D
RIT.
E
A TEMPO

SHENANDOAH

ADAGIO ♩ = 68

ARR. LLUIS GÓMEZ

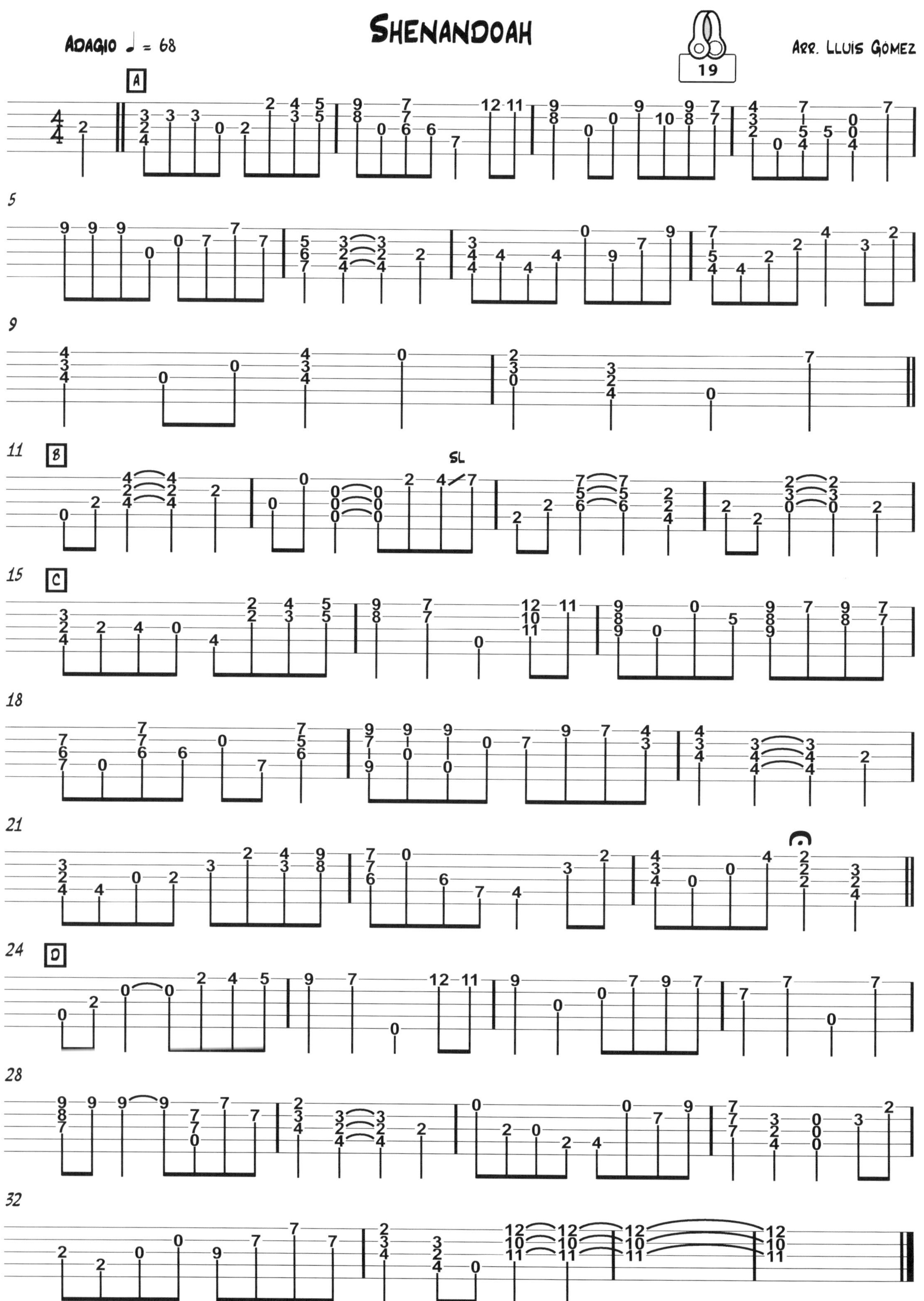

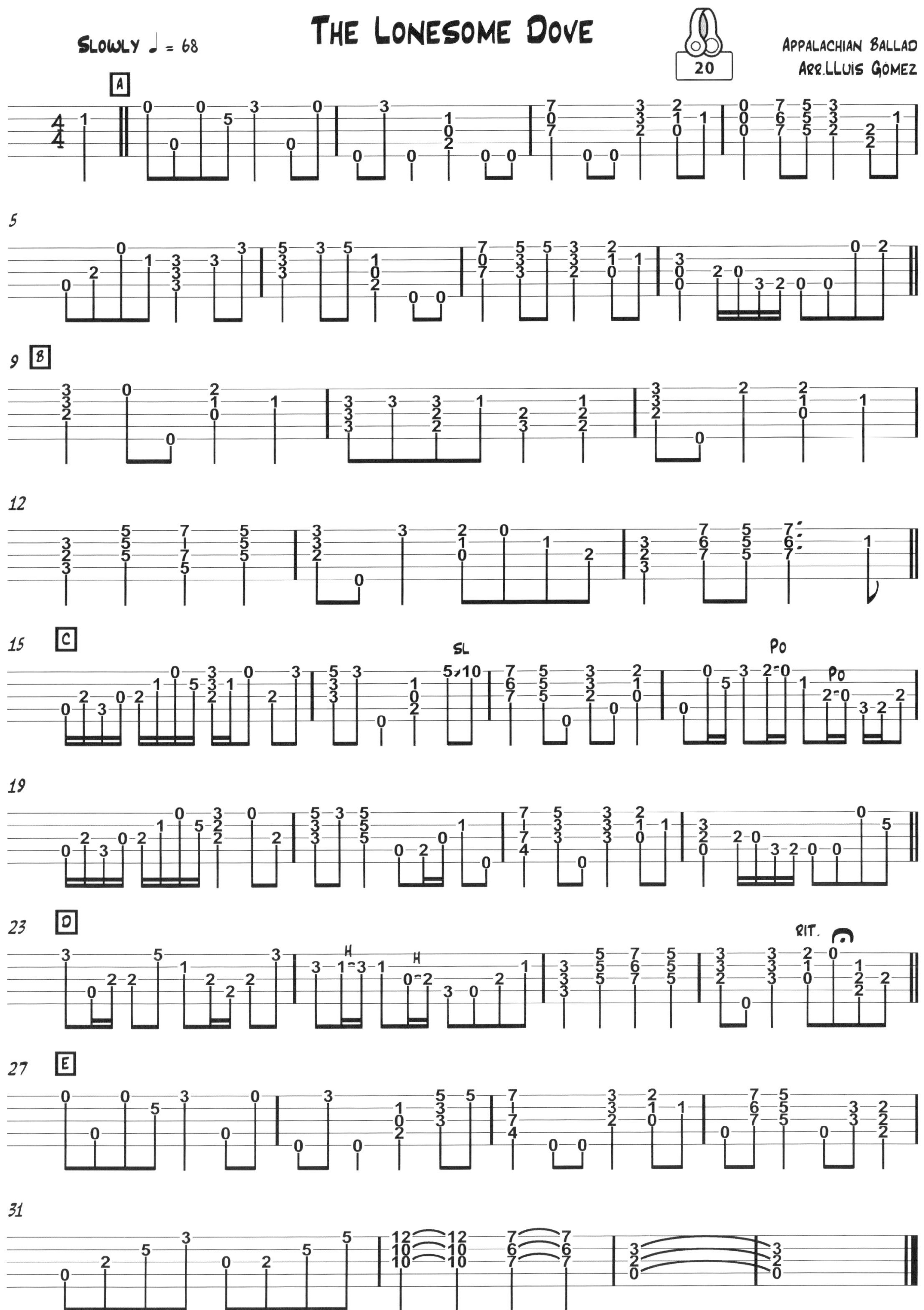

The Lonesome Dove
Slowly ♩ = 68
20
Appalachian Ballad
Arr.Lluis Gomez
A
B
C
D
E
SL
PO
H
RIT.

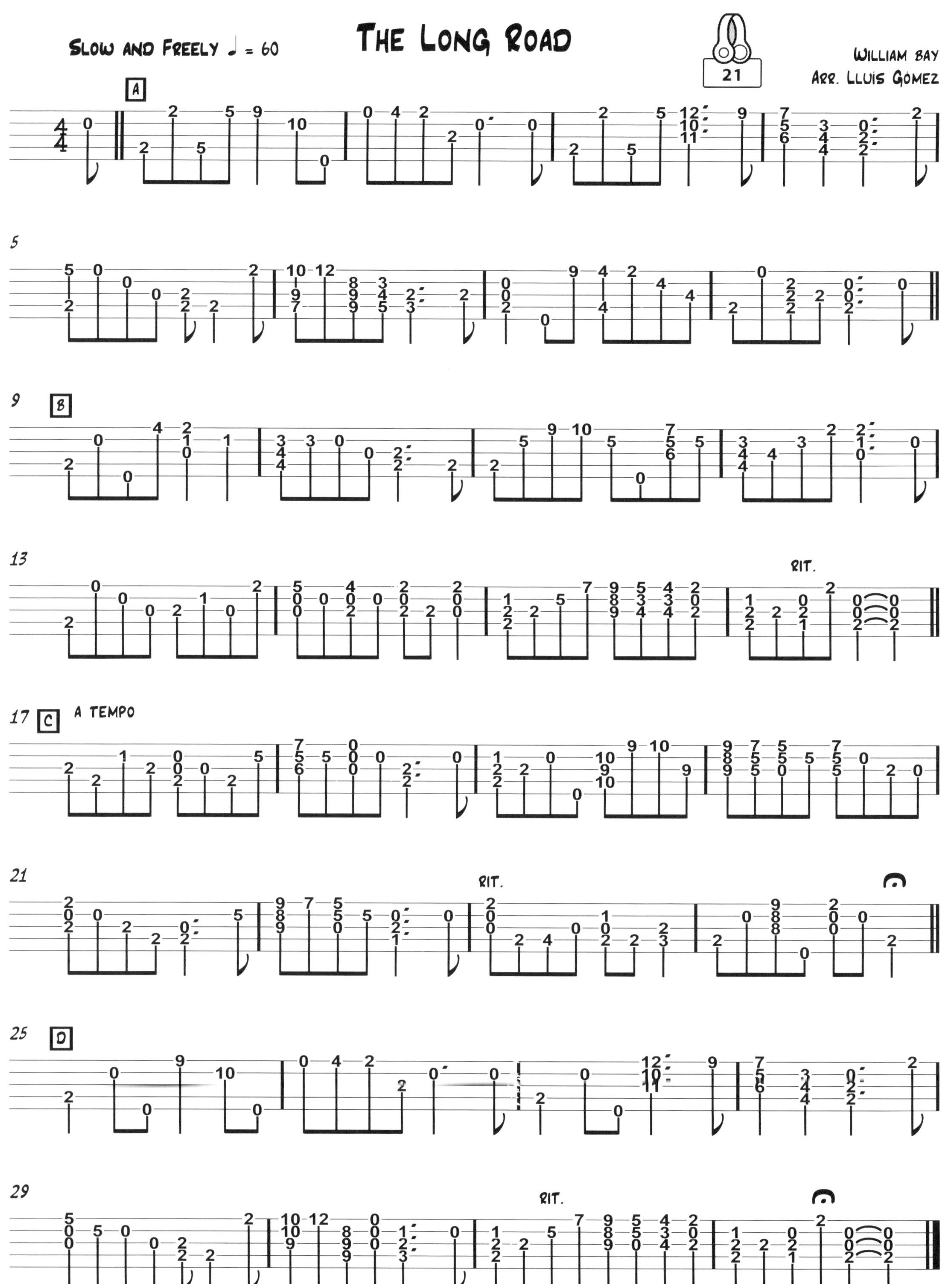
The Long Road
Slow and Freely ♩ = 60
21
William Bay
Arr. Lluis Gomez
A
B
rit.
C
A tempo
rit.
D
rit.

This page has been left blank to avoid an awkward page turn.

THE OLD COUNTRY

22

WILLIAM BAY
ARR. LLUIS GÓMEZ

GENTLY ♩ = 110

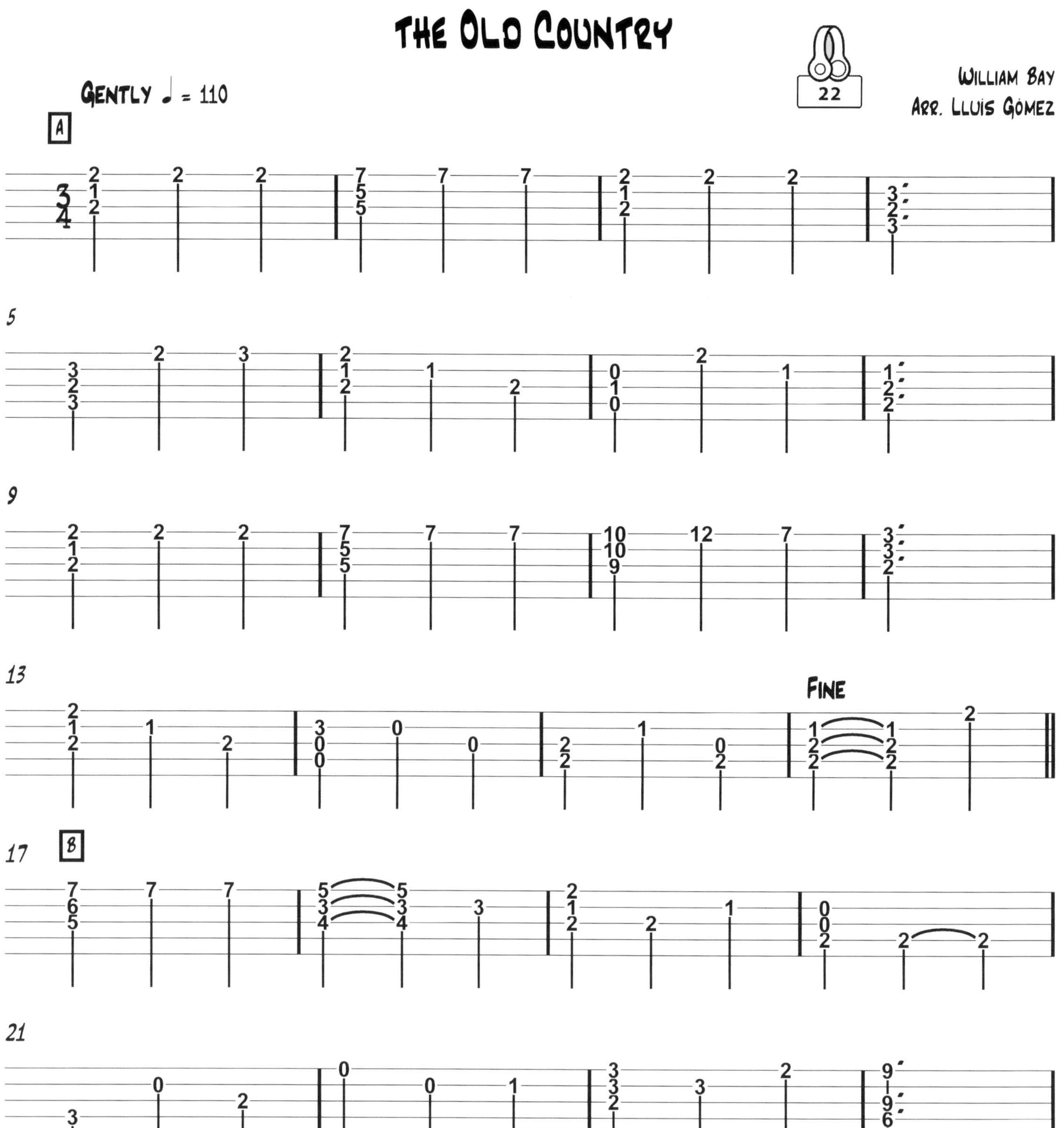

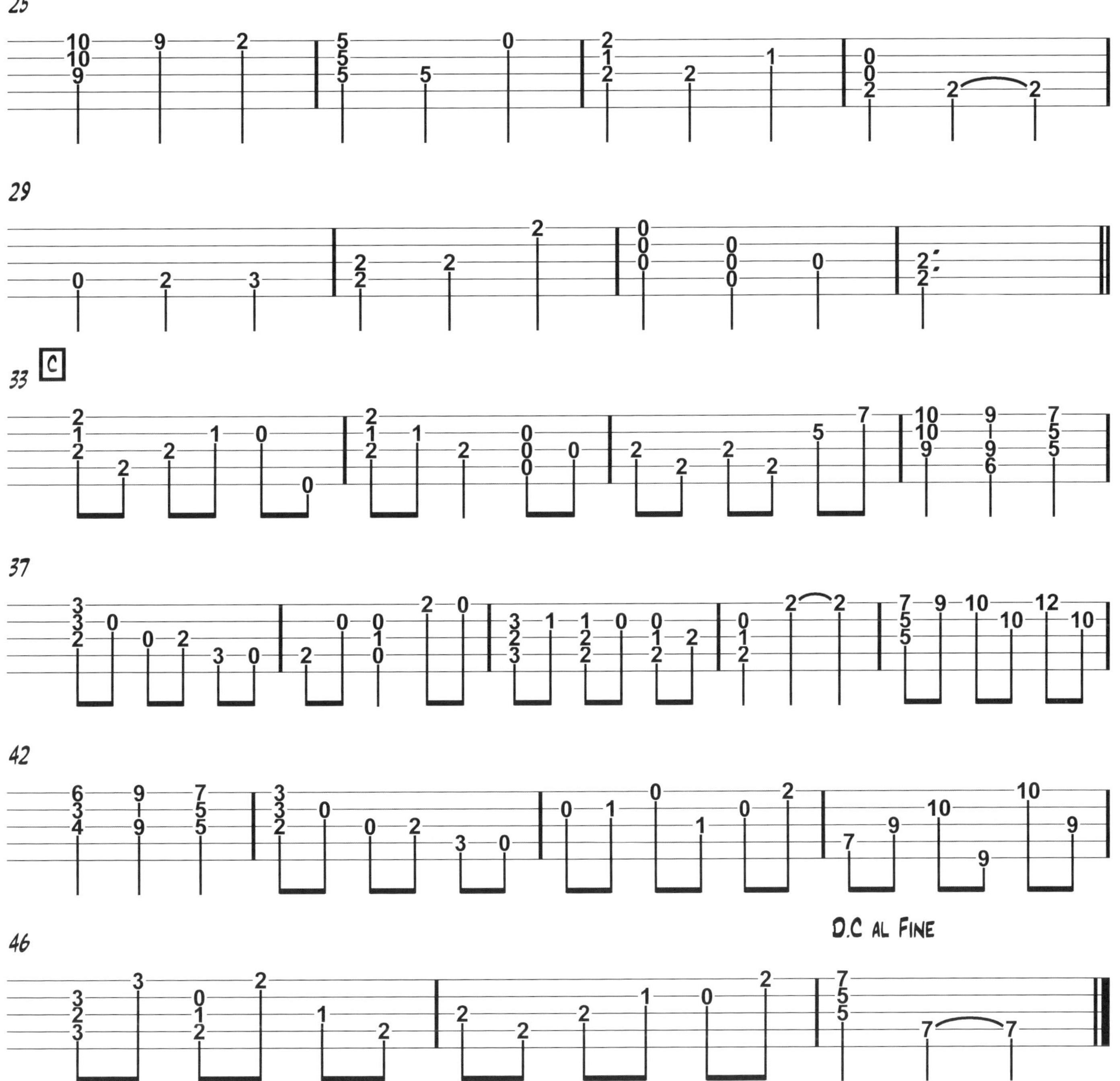
25
29
33
C
37
42
46
D.C al Fine

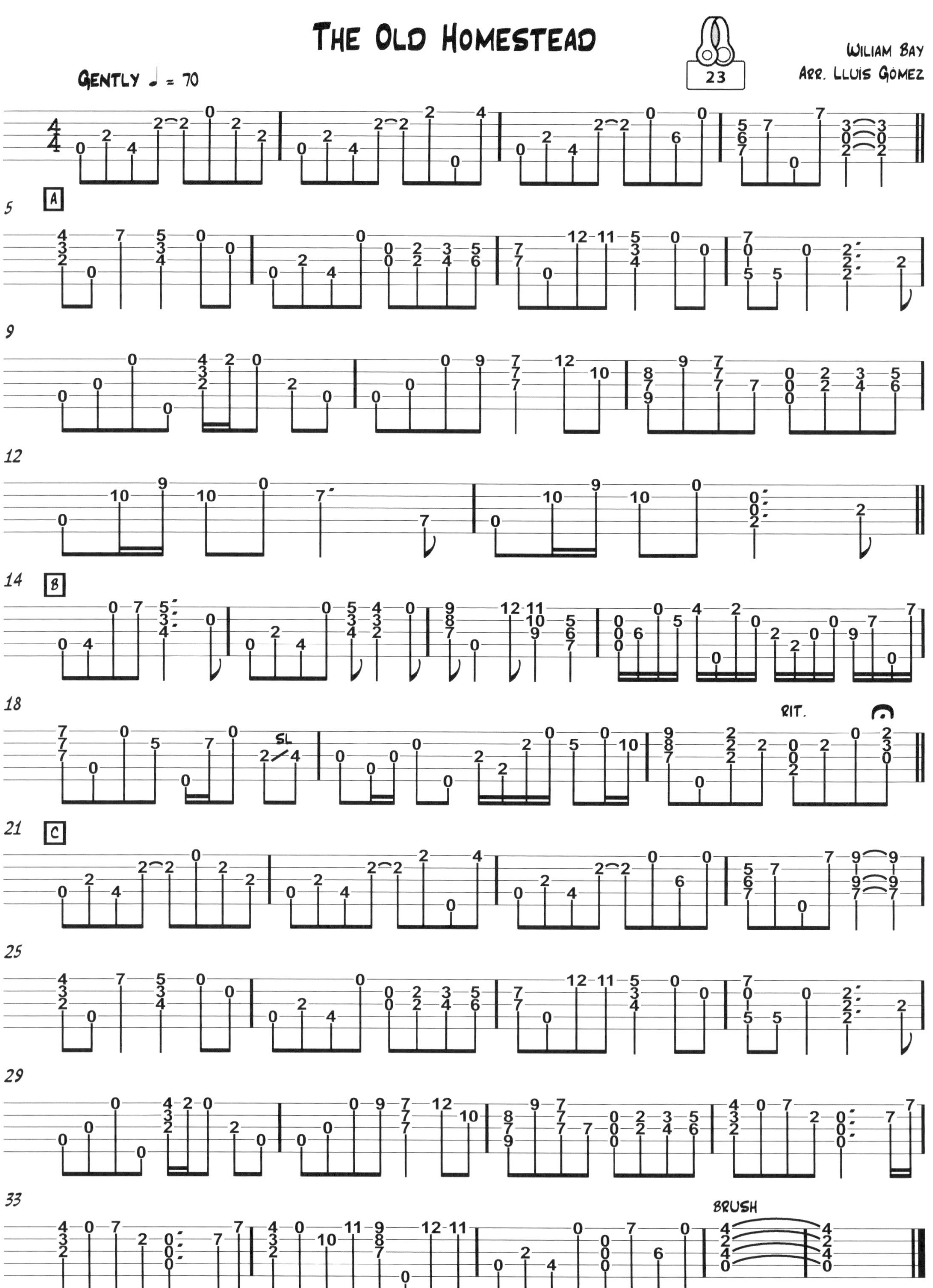
The Old Homestead
23
Wiliam Bay
Arr. Lluis Gómez
Gently ♩ = 70
A
B
SL
RIT.
C
BRUSH

To a Wild Rose

Slowly and Freely ♩ = 62

24

Edward MacDowell
Arr. by Lluis Gómez

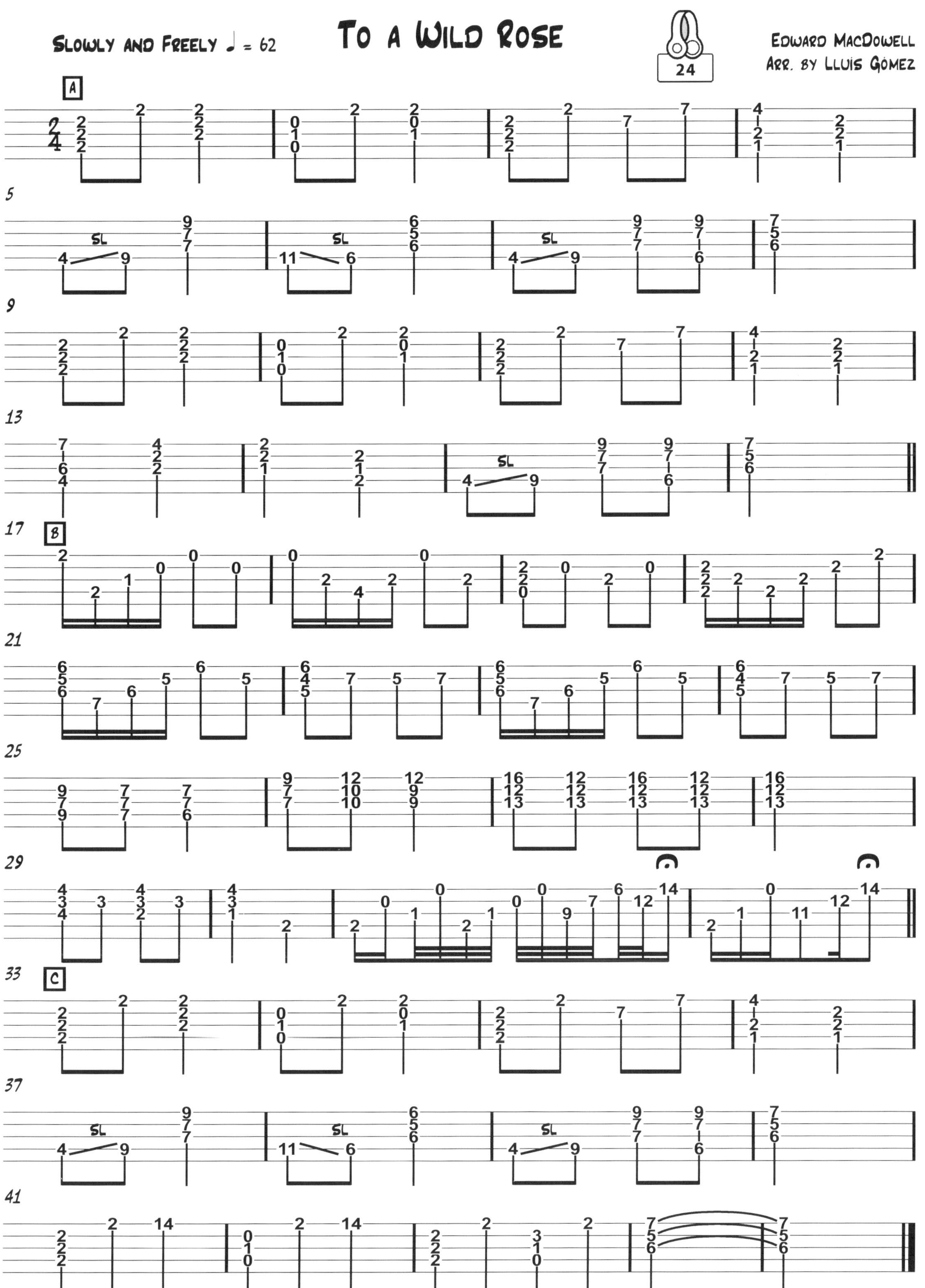

Trail of Tears

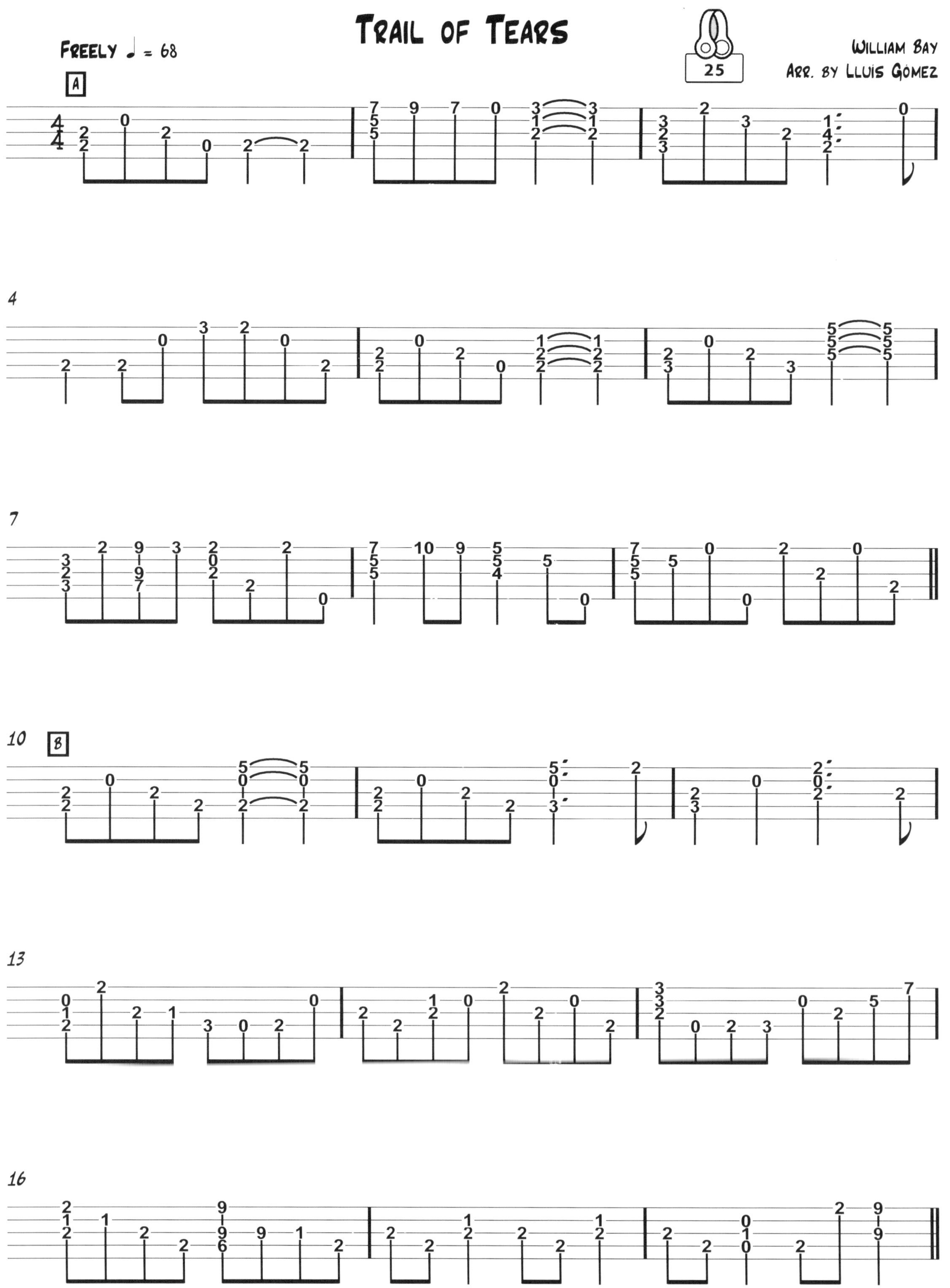

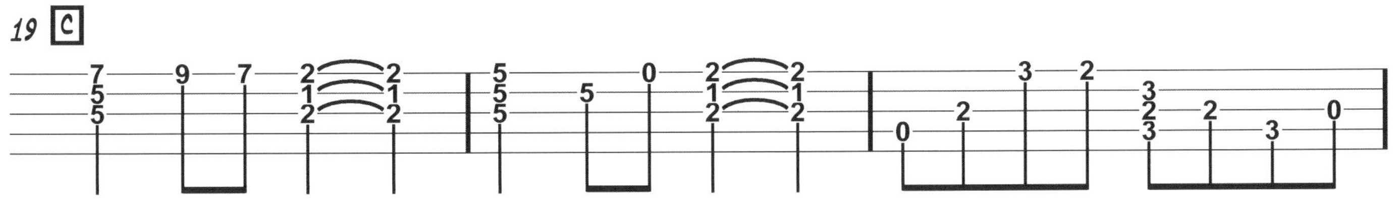
19
C

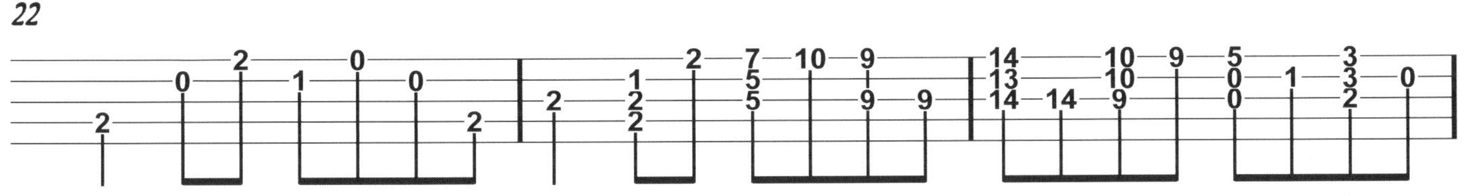
22

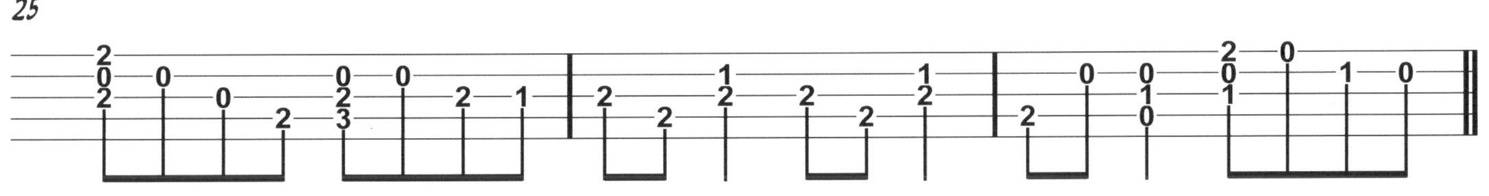
25

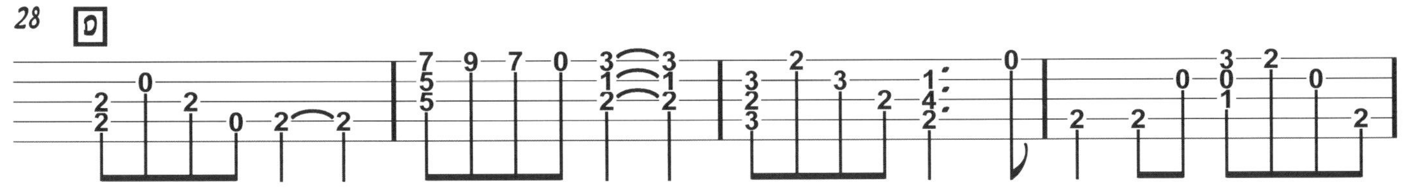
28
D

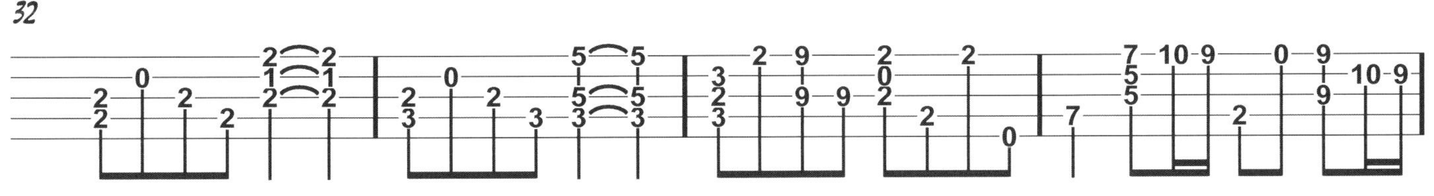
32

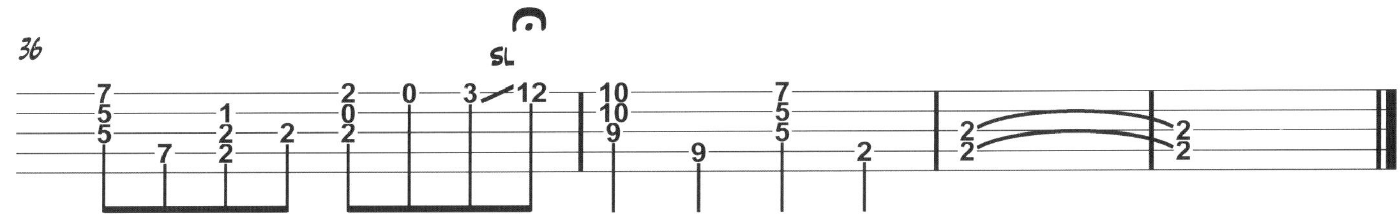
36
SL

Lluís Gómez

At an early age, largely encouraged by the musical atmosphere in his family, Lluís Gómez started teaching himself the acoustic guitar and electric bass. He studied the flute for two years and at the age of 18 went on to study classical guitar with Pere Payes at the Music School of Premià de Mar, and subsequently took up the electric guitar with Josep Traver. He also studied modern harmony with Ramón Montoliu at Badalona's Municipal School of Music. At the age of 30 he began learning the fiddle, self-taught at first, and later studying with Raúl Munizaga.

The discovery of bluegrass through the 1975 *Banjo Paris Session* album was a watershed in his career. He was so taken by this style that he immediately picked up the 5-string banjo and sought lessons from Sedo Garcia and Ricky Araiza in Barcelona. He then travelled to France, Ireland, the United Kingdom, and the United States to take lessons from Jean Marie Redon, Bill Keith, Tony Trischka, Pete Wernick, Noam Pikelny, Adam Larrabee, and Jayme Stone among others.

Since 2020, Lluís has been involved in a Zoom group called "The Flatheads" with banjo players such as Jake Schepps, Adam Larrabee, Hank Smith, Nat Torkington, Tony Trischka, Béla Fleck, and others where they discuss various banjo techniques. In addition, he has been an assistant teacher under Béla Fleck at the prestigious Blue Ridge Banjo Camp at the Brevard Music Center in North Carolina where he has taught flamenco banjo workshops.

Lluís has performed and recorded extensively with many artists and bands, always on the folk scene but also in a wide range of styles from flamenco to pop and rock music; he has also recorded the music for several films and performed live on the theater stage as an actor/musician. Widely acknowledged as a performer both at home and abroad, Lluís has recorded multiple CDs of original material.

He is also known as one of the great connoisseurs and leading promoters of bluegrass music in Spain. Lluís directs the Bluegrass and Old-Time Music Festival, *Al Ras* as well as The Barcelona Bluegrass Camp, and teaches banjo, mandolin, and fiddle at various schools in the Barcelona region and abroad, among them the prestigious International Stage Musique Acoustique Campus in Belgium. He somehow finds the time to play in several bluegrass, folk, and jazz manouche bands and hosts a bluegrass jam session in Barcelona.

Lluís has written several methods on how to play the 5-string banjo, including a bilingual Spanish-Catalan book in collaboration with multi-instrumentalist singer-songwriter, Toni Giménez. He regularly writes for several specialized magazines and in March 2015, he was featured on the cover of the prestigious *Banjo Newsletter* magazine.

As Lluís also plays mandolin and violin he is the co-author with Oriol Saña of *The Bluegrass Violin* written in English and Spanish. Lluís is the sole author of *Fun Solos to Play*, *Early Music Gems*, *An Early American Christmas*, and *Christmas in the British Isles*—all for the 5-string banjo and published by Mel Bay Publications.